MW01088048

August 4, 2023

Dearest friend Hasan,

What an amazing 50+ year greatness journey we have shared.

BRING INNER GREATNESS OUT

With many more years to come.
Love
Dr. Mansur Hasib

BRING INNER GREATNESS OUT

Personal Brand

DR. MANSUR HASIB

Tomorrow's Strategy Today, LLC

ABOUT THE BOOK

Why do movie actors, singers, TV anchors, and athletes earn millions of dollars? Why are they paid more than their managers? Why do they get sponsorships from companies unrelated to their field? Could you become globally famous in your own field? Would you like to have multiple streams of income?

Do you create your own success? Are you prepared for a layoff? Do you define your job in your own image? Would you lose your identity if you lost your job? How do you negotiate compensation? Are you prepared for job interviews? Why are you the best candidate for this job? What are your salary requirements? Would you like to be more effective at networking? What is the best way to search for jobs that are not even advertised? Why are people far less qualified than you always getting that job or that promotion that you wanted?

If any of these questions are swirling in your mind, this book has your answers. You will be amazed at the rapid results you will experience.

Published in the United States of America
Available in print, ebook, and author narrated audiobook
Order signed books for shipment within USA, view educational content, and contact for speaking requests:
www.cybersecurityleadership.com

"**A Field Guide for Perfecting Your Uniqueness** - For those unfamiliar with his work, Dr. Mansur Hasib is a well-respected influencer in the field of cybersecurity. His renowned style of public speaking and leadership draws people in which makes him a highly sought after mentor. The book is a reflection of experiences and lessons that span Dr. Hasib's career. Through the lense of a life-long learner, his decorum and level of professionalism provides readers with the necessary resources to design their own plan for developing a personal brand and bringing their inner greatness out. Whether or not a reader has prior knowledge of personal branding, there is something for everyone to learn or be reminded of in a way that allows for patience, and grace at a pace that does not overwhelm." - **Angelina Simms**, USA, November 2, 2020

"**Personal Branding Is A Must!** - Dr. Hasib certainly has a way with words! Very good read. I especially like Chapters 3 & 8. What he mentions about personal branding versus organizational branding is something that most people fail to consider. I've witnessed peers assuming that their organization would support their efforts when trying to make a name for themselves in the field, but it didn't work out that way. Sometimes, even if you've partnered up with that company, they may still never support you, unless there is a way in which they also benefit from the exposure, which typically comes at a cost. I like to call this "piggyback" branding, as they're taking your ideas, your marketing, your advertisements, etc., and using it against you so that it benefits them, mainly because they "allowed" you to mention their name in a post, or post on a flyer, etc. It happens more than people may realize in Cyber, and in the end, the organization WINS. Way to go with this book Dr. Hasib! I've very much so enjoyed all of the personal stories shared, along with the excellent advice that was provided for the readers!" - **Katoria Henry**, USA, November 2, 2020

"Dr. Mansur Hasib's Personal Brand is a game changer - Bring Inner Greatness Out: Personal Brand" is the skill we must all master in our life-time, whether be for our personal satisfaction, for our family or for our career benefit. The sooner you do it, the more success you will achieve. You will truly achieve more success than you ever imagined possible. You get a step by step guide how to do everything with plenty of stories and examples including Dr. Hasib's own personal story of success as well as his students and mentees. I have personally observed him in action in person. However, after I read the book, the methodology became crystal clear to me. I knew Dr. Hasib has his own model of personal branding that I have never seen before. In this book I saw why. I am so happy he chose to share his secrets with the world. This book is meant to be read many times as a career guide. Even if you get the paperback, you may still want to have the ebook with you all the time so you can refer to it and also share ideas with friends. You can also use the book as a group study and practice tool. Give it as a gift for your family and friends for this upcoming holidays. They will thank you for it. I plan to buy more to give away as gifts myself." - **Rima Aristocrat**, Canada, November 7, 2020

"All of us are born unique and exceptional. Yet, too many of us spend a lifetime blending in and staying average. - Very rarely would I start a book review with a quote, but that is a phenomenal opening that sets the scene for this book. Our personal brand is worth far more than we realise. And for that reason, it is worth investing in. This book provides all the tips and tricks for how to grow a personal brand. Our own brand should always be more than any one position we hold. The book highlights the need for modern and flexible practices to be utilised within recruit-ment, reward and retention...." Full review at: https://www.cybersecurity-professionals.com/post/bring-inner-greatness-out-a-review, - **Emma Garland**, UK, December 11, 2020

"You Are More Than Your Job Title, Build Your Personal Brand - Dr. Hasib's Bring Inner Greatness Out book ensures readers are ready to build their personal brand. There are a few chapters that resonated with me. In Chapter 1, Why Build A Personal Brand- This chapter really spoke to me. Due to being unemployed for nine months from 2018-2019. I had realized I was really just about my current role and what I did at work every day. I did not have anything else to fall on. A Personal Brand. During that time of "finding myself," I established a personal brand by sharing my story dealing with the Cybersecurity Workforce. Dr. Hasib mentions some benefits that I surely can agree with. - Increase your value of work - Market Your Ideas Better - Create multiple sources of income. In Chapter 3, What Is Personal Brand? This is an important chapter for anyone that is stuck with finding out who they are. For instance, I'm currently a System Engineer. However, when I introduce myself to cybersecurity professionals or if you follow me on Linkedin. My branding and the way I display my name is Katia Dean, voiceofcyberpros. I earned the voiceofcyberpros due to speaking up about the issues dealing with the Cybersecurity Workforce. In Chapter 8 I was honored that he shared my personal experince with Pearsonal Branding. Thanks to Dr. Hasib for his guidance along the way and assisting me with building my personal brand. With his advice I was able to get out of shell and author my 1st ebook. Anyone that is reading this book remember you are more than your job title! Get out there and establish your own personal brand and grow in your career. I also recommend his other book as well Cybersecurity Leadership!" - **Katia Dean**, #voiceofcyberpros, USA, December 13, 2020

"**Dr. Mansur Hasib covers personal branding techniques and tips in "Bring Inner Greatness Out: Personal Brand.** He shares approaches on a variety of subjects including communications, collaboration, speaking, trade shows, writing, and digital media such as audio and video. Dr. Hasib covers practical examples, sharing what he learned from publishing a book included in the cybersecurity canon and the Cybersecurity People's Choice Award. This book includes helpful techniques and lessons learned that help the reader bring inner greatness out!. Dr. Hasib includes pictures and advice of students and collaborators. Well done!" - **Dr. Jeff Daniels,** USA, January 30, 2021

"**Identify your value** - Dr. Hasib is a man whose passion in life is to help others and in my opinion wrote this book with one goal in mind -- to specifically help you grow and excel in your life's journey by helping you bring out your inner greatness. "What is inner greatness?" Greatness is the value proposition that you bring to anything you do. It's the reason an employer will choose\hire you (your brand) instead of someone else (the competing brand). Identifying inner greatness and a personal brand is essential to your life! The author reminds us of "one important question every employer asks: is the value of this person higher than what I will pay for the person?" How will you answer that question should the employer be referencing you? If you want the answer to be you, then start your journey today by purchasing a copy of this book. Dr. Hasib provides stories and identifies steps on how YOU can bring out your inner greatness and build your personal brand. The book has helped me and I'm confident that the book will help you to bring out your inner greatness leading you to develop your personal brand. Get the book today and start developing a name brand that companies will compete with each other to hire you." - **Stanley McCluskey**, USA, February 21, 2021

Personal Gift, to consolidate the inner Greatness in Me and to expose my brand. Great job as always - I had a great time listening to Dr. Mansur's Audio book "Bring Inner Greatness Out: Personal Brand." Its worth is unmeasurable. Thanks to Dr. Mansur for this lifetime gift. Detailed review: https://www.linkedin.com/pulse/bring-inner-greatness-out-personal-brand-birthday-gift-bishakha-jain. - **Bishakha Jain**, India, March 6, 2021

"What a powerful opportunity to learn! - I am truly grateful for your composing this guidebook for personal branding. I must say it is right on time as I proceed in launching my company. Section 3.5 Your Mission in Life & Section 6 resonates to my core. I am changing the game with my passion and encourage others that are willing to step into their own greatness to not only get the book, but to take notes and enjoy the journey. Thank you again for your endeavors on this project!" - **Ron W. Brown, Sr.**, USA, February 26, 2021

"A guide to personal and career success - I have found Dr. Hasib's second book as spectacular as the first one. I got to know Dr. Hasib while studying for a Master's program where he was serving as a program chair. He led his students to success with most of the principles and concepts that are discussed in this book. Besides being a program chair and a professor at the University, Dr. Hasib was a mentor for many who tirelessly invests his time in his students. In addition to his distinct approaches and methodologies in academia, he is widely known for helping students to improve their communication and personal skills. This book defines who Dr. Hasib is as a human being, mentor, and academic person. Everything written in this book is what he used as a tool to change many of his students' lives. Most students within the cybersecurity program he chaired benefited from his mentorship. Students were able to determine their self-worth in the job market, identify core values and missions, build personal brands, and gain better control of their careers. It is my belief that this book will motivate and guide readers to discover, develop, leverage, and protect personal brands." - **Fasil Abera,** USA, March 5, 2021

"Be recognised for your value - Dr. Mansur Hasib's purpose in life is to 'help people succeed' and it shines throughout this book. It is full of practical examples of how he has helped bring out the greatness in his students. He backs it up with his own stories about building his personal brand, which has led to countless awards and global recognition as a keynote speaker and author. Use this book to build your personal brand and get your audience seeking the value you provide." - **Brian Donovan,** Australia, March 12, 2021

"Authentic and from the heart! - Dr. Mansur Hasib certainly has a way with words to not only convey a message but also the authenticity and passion behind it. It's hard to pick my favorite chapter, section or phrase but if I absolutely had to, I'd say Chapter 8 - Developing my personal brand, Section 8.2 - My values. Being someone who is passionate about leading from the heart, every phrase in this book was igniting that passion further as I played and replayed the audio. Dr. Mansur Hasib has shown me the way forward to building my personal brand. Bless his heart! Also, I normally don't go for audio books but I wouldn't do it differently for any audio book narrated by Dr. Mansur Hasib! Thank you, Dr. Mansur Hasib for sharing your knowledge, experiences and passion for developing others!!" - **Shirley Lemus,** USA, March 16, 2021

"Choose to be average or choose to be great - Dr. Hasib is brilliant. I met Dr. Hasib at the 2019 (ISC2) Conference in Orlando, Florida. My daughter was being honored with the Up and Coming Information Security Professional of the Year Award. An award she never would have received had it not been for Dr. Hasib and his mentoring. His book is right on the mark. I gave it to my seventeen year old nephew who is on the verge of reaching his inner greatness. A young person would definitely benefit from reading this book. A person can choose to be average and mediocre or they can choose to be great. Dr. Hasib's book takes you step by step on how to become great and how to build your personal brand. Dr. Hasib will mention my daughter throughout his book, and how he guided her to inner greatness. Before meeting Dr. Hasib, she was very shy. I highly recommend this book to anyone who chooses to be great in their field and to build their personal brand." - **Arletta Evans**, USA, March 21, 2021

"**Show Up Fully!** - I loved Dr. Hasib's book "Cybersecurity Leadership" and happened upon a LinkedIn introduction to the concepts from his new book "Bring Inner Greatness Out: Personal Brand." It was a pleasure to meet several presenters who clearly had benefited from his teachings of Personal Branding! Their energy and uniquely individual styles of story telling was inspirational. That very night, I updated my LinkedIn page with personalized background and added featured examples of my public work. Immediately, I received more of the professional traffic that I desired. This book avoids jargon and is filled with real world examples of how you can express your unique value to employers and world. I have listened to Section 8 numerous times. It includes the topics: My Value, Bios and Professional Pictures, Cross-Brand Promotion, Global Networking, and Earned Media. This book literally changed my life and will continue to as I work through other chapters. Following Dr. Hasib's examples, I collaborated on a podcast, contributed to a national security blog, and was approached to speak at a Global Women in Tech Summit. Your results may vary, but I doubt it was a coincidence. Dr. Hasib's passion for coaching, and mentoring really shines in this book. My next goal is mastering Section 10!" - **Melissa S. Vice**, USA, March 31, 2021

"**Great book** - I purchased outside of Amazon, but this is a great book on why you need a personal brand. My personal brand has led to a VP position. Buy this book if you want to take your life to the next level." - **Ken Underhill,** USA, March 31, 2021

"**Discover Yourself with this book** - I will not rate the success of this book with words like "The best book ever" because this book brought to me much more than that. If you are lost amidst the competition of performing better than others in terms of numbers, this book is for you. What we have been graded on up till now has nothing to do with what can be achieved with our own values, because that inner greatness is still waiting to be discovered within us. Simplicity of words used to deliver a great message like this is the true beauty of this book. My two important takeaways from this book are: 1. Greatness is a choice. 2. The pursuit for greatness never ends. And what's more? Riding on the journey of defining our own personal brand with Dr. Mansur Hasib himself." - **Anushka Lal,** India, April 7, 2021

"**I do not usually read non-fiction,** but Dr Hasib was kind enough to give me an audiobook copy of his work for free. I was not familiar with his other work prior to this, but it was definitely eye-opening. I think this is very important advice for anyone with something to sell or to share with the world. It will change the way you think of marketing and getting your work out there. It may even change the way you think about yourself." - **Ellie Jay**, UK, April 11, 2021

"**If you have the drive, this is the recipe for success!** - Dr. Mansur Hasib has done it again. His passion of helping others succeed is unmatched in my eyes. This book give you a roadmap to being the best you that you can be. Everything from dressing for success to what equipment he uses to produce his audiobooks. There are two things you need to do, 1. Buy and read the book to gain the knowledge he has provided and 2. Have the passion or desire to put in motion in your own life. This exact roadmap may not work for everyone, however, using this as a baseline takes most of the leg work out of the equation. He has provided it for you. His willingness to share his experiences with us portrays his desire to help others. Thank you Dr. Mansur Hasib for another excellent book. Respectfully," - **Thomas Bishop**, USA, April 17, 2021

"**An outstanding book for improving your personal brand** - I really love this book. It is informative and easy and simple to understand. I bought the kindle version for myself and then Dr Mansur Hasib kindly provided me with the Audible version for free. This book is helpful for people who want to improve. It starts off by making you think about what your values are, then goes more into what is your personal brand, why do you need a personal brand then goes through how to build your personal brand. I particularly like how it covers practical examples which I have followed. Communication skills is a weakness of mine and a section in this book recommended joining Toastmasters to improve in this area. I recently joined my local Toastmasters club and have just completed my first ice-breaker. This book also made me think about myself and how I want to be presented. It talks about your values and how it affects your brand. Plus, it also suggests how to use your personal brand and ensure that you are consistent between your social media accounts and LinkedIn and your cv. Finally, I want to talk about the author. I am familiar with Dr Mansur Hasib since I work in cybersecurity and he wrote an excellent book on cybersecurity leadership about 10 years ago. He is very approachable, and he wants to help people to improve. He was the narrator for the audible version and the pace of the book was excellent, it allowed me to think about the words as well as listen to them. An outstanding book." - **Jason Medhurst**, UK, April 18, 2021

"**Timely, compelling, and riveting** - Needs better orientation for your carrier path? Dr. Mansur Hasib has written a Masterpiece of practical counsel for you. 'Bring Inner Greatness Out' shows exactly how you can build a personal brand, achieve success and freedom while owning your own business. This book is a priceless gift for everyone. It has encouraged me to independently publish my own book. It is timely, compelling, and riveting." - **Dr. Dennis Okui,** CISSP, MCSE, CSM, Professor & Author, USA, April 20, 2021

"**The Total Greatness Package for Personal Success** - Dr. Mansur has put together a powerful book that was written well and performed well. This book is for anyone that is looking to advance in their career and life because of the powerful points Dr. Mansur made like: Don't let one company monopolize my skills. The 3 skills for unleashing your greatness...Leadership, Listening, and Public Speaking. The unconventional thing to do while you are looking for a new job and or next opportunity. This book on personal branding should be required reading (and listening) for any career professional or entrepreneur. It's also a book that you must go back to because there are so many nuggets and ideas that you can apply immediately." - **Dom Brightmon**, Bestselling Author & Host of the Going North Podcast, USA, April 26, 2021

"**Everyone has a talent. Find it and make it shine!** - This is a book about personal branding which is relevant these days. It becomes harder to believe in ourselves and finding our place in this fast-paced world. I learned a lot of new stuff to continue my book publishing journey! I recommend it for reading to people who have big career dreams and need more clarity and guidance." - **Lubov Leonova**, Canada, May 11, 2021

"**Excellent in every way** - This is the book to own if you need advice and inspiration for developing your personal brand. What is a personal brand? Why is it important? How do you develop one? What do you do with it once it is developed? All that is covered in great detail by Dr. Hasib, as well as other aspects of developing and projecting personal greatness. Listening to this book made me excited to put into practice the advice he offers. These words are a must for anybody wanting to present their best self to the world." - **Jim Larsen**, USA, May 16, 2021

"**Wake up call** -Thank you for helping me to look at my brand critically. Time to reboot and build right." - **Charles Karanja**, UK, June 9, 2021

"**Dare to bring it out** - What can I say? Intelligent, informative, inspiring???. I hope as I have picked up on improving my personal brand, so does my teen daughter who was listening in the background. Regardless of the Cybersecurity background of the author, this book is definitely for all ages, never too young or too old to pick up on positive and empowering ideas to bring out your inner greatness. A book to be re-read 📖 Thank you Dr Hasib." - **Kiren Sohpal**, UK, June 24, 2021

"**Both Books together will Set an Amazing Path** - Listening to both books has been an awesome experience of my life. Integrating the two gave me a sense of respect for myself and others by exercising leadership and building my brand at the same time. People know me as a charismatic, caring, and unselfish person with my own individuality at work and outside of work. I highly recommend both books! Thanks #DrCybersecurity! Sincerely, The #CyberRapper," - **Tomiko K. Evans**, USA, July 10, 2021

"**Motivational for employees in any career to move on up!!!** - Both of these books are extremely impressive and I would recommend both of them!!!! Dr. Mansur Hasib, who I am so fortunate to know and be taught by, is such an inspiration and motivator that I honestly think any person looking towards leadership and/or personal growth in their professional lives would benefit exponentially in their journey from reading these books! Whether you are an elementary education teacher, an engineer, a receptionist, or Cybersecurity field -you have a LOT To gain from these books which underlying themes apply across all career paths in my opinion. Dr. Hasib frames relationship, roles, and values of employees to employers in such a unique way that it revitalized my understanding of my true value to the organizations I have worked for. Bigger picture through nutshells and fascinating stories!!!" - **Elena Healing**, USA, July 11, 2021

"I had the privilege to listen to the book Bring Inner Greatness Out - This book is a true mine of gold as it is a practical guide to guide whoever wants to transform his/her life and become a better version by bringing the inner greatness out: a leader in all the aspect of the life especially professionally. Thank you Dr. Mansur Hasib for making this book that everyone should read and or listen. Moreover, the audio version of the book is incredible given the quality of the voice and the articulation of the words." - **William Fotseu**, Canada, August 13, 2021

"Build your own success and income - Dr Hasib brings his vast experience to tackle the multiple interconnected issues of tackling exploitation, bad managers, self-esteem, income, independence, personal happiness and recognition. He actively encourages everyone to be kind, thoughtful and to develop their skills to the utmost. His makes incredibly valuable suggestions and real-world examples to navigate the modern world and also become financially independent. This book is an essential read for everyone." - **Dr. Mike Brass**, UK, August 17, 2021

"Be The Best Version of Yourself! - Dr. Mansur Hasib is a well-respected leader in Cybersecurity. Also, known as Dr. Cybersecurity, he is a great mentor to many, including myself, world renowned author, and speaker. When reading his book, he focuses on how to establish your personal brand ranging from your name leading to your inner greatness? What is it? A talent that is unique to you. Feeling empowered, inspired and confident, Bringing Your Inner Greatness out discusses various ways to establish and maintain your personal branding and to believe in yourself. No matter if you have no previous knowledge of what personal branding is to re branding, Bringing Your Inner Greatness Out is a great book for all levels of personal branding." - **Aisha Berry**, USA, August 23, 2021

"More than a penny for your thoughts! It is more like a Proven Power Plan For Platinum Performance - Is a penny valuable? Some may answer that question with a resounding "Yes! – pennies are building blocks of wealth". Others may casually dismiss the small coin and say, "No, a penny is minute and trivial, not worth any effort to stoop and collect." Consider a visual spectrum of quantity represented by a horizontal line – on one end is $0 and on the opposing end is $1,000,000. Any amount along the spectrum is representative of value, regardless of how high or low the amount is, and any influence(s) upon increasing that value would be considered [a] valuable. Which penny is the most valuable among the one hundred million pennies required to amass $1,000,000? The very first one that begins the journey from nothing to one? A few to several? How about the very last one that facilitates crossing the threshold into "millionaire status"? Or, would it be best to say each one-cent piece possesses its own, unique value and contributes to the greater totality? That would be my persuasion. A tiny penny can have an accumulating effect of great magnitude as it relates to wealth. In similar fashion each rudimentary piece of your individuality can have an exponential effect increasing value within the lives of others both personally and professionally. Dr. Hasib's book Bring Inner Greatness Out: Personal Brand is not only a tremendous value of theoretical and practical knowledge regarding how to build a personal brand but also an invaluable reinforcement of understanding coupled with expertise as to why you must build, maintain, and protect your personal brand. Dr. Hasib masterfully directs your focus to the treasure(s) within yourself; he is passionate in his effort to bring out your greatness, for therein is the purest, most effective value. The book is easy to read, congruent in its theme, and immediately applicable. It is very unfortunate that a majority of "help" books and articles are written from the perspective that greatness is somewhere "out there", and you must find it. No, the truth is that greatness is already within you; it must be perfected and released "out there". Read the book; heed the book. Thank you and Very Well Done, Dr. Hasib!" - **Jesse R. J. Qurollo**, USA, August 23, 2021

"Changed My Life - I just finished the Audible version of Dr. Mansur Hasib's (#DrCybersecurity) book Bring Inner Greatness Out. It was transformative. I have searched for what I want to be when I grow up (whenever that's going to happen) my entire life. My childhood dreams took me to flying, which was awesome. Then I had a family, and my priorities changed. So I went into cybersecurity. I got an MBA and studied for CISSP. But I did middle management in the Air Force and I can't stand meetings (especially when they could be emails, or emails that could be text messages #millennial). .. I have been teaching for about 3 years now. I started while I was in the Air Force, teaching Introduction to Special Operations at the Air Force Special Operations School. Other than the flying aspects, I was learning a lot of it as I was teaching. Nothing is that complicated, so it all comes down to teaching ability, which anyone can learn if they care to. I like it. So, when I got out of the military in 2020 and chanced my way into teaching cybersecurity, I hit the jackpot, although I didn't realize it for a few months (or a year #whatever). I love teaching. I do something cool and then help other people do it, too. My specialty is offensive cyber, hacking, pentesting, threat emulation, whatever you want to call it. I learned a lot of my technique from YouTube and reasonably-priced, amazing online courses. I'm not as handsome as those guys, but I get what they're doing. I teach it in my classes. Maybe I can put together some Youtube videos of the stuff I'm doing. So, I made a YT channel . I also started posting relevant resources I've used for certification, getting a job, transitioning out of the military, or just learning more stuff to be better at my job. People seem to dig it. Then I read .. and realized that I have a brand. I have a brand whether I mean to or not. When people think of my name, they think of something (hopefully good things #needy). So, if there's going to be a brand either way, am I controlling it? Am I utilizing my brand the way I want to? Does my brand hold value? Am I valuing it properly, myself? What am I giving away for free? Am I devaluing my brand? What is the effect of my brand in the ecosystem? These are all the questions I asked myself while going through the book. Dr. Mansur Hasib shared personal stories and experiences from his career and his students and mentees. That part really put into perspective the realities of my brand. This has helped me solidify many of my choices and make decisions for my near future. It has helped me be more purposeful in my LinkedIn posts and my YouTube channel going forward. If you are creating content in any format (even if you're coming up with your own ideas at your job), then you need to start thinking about your brand and what you're doing with it. Go get this book. It's super reasonably priced and well worth your time to get direction, inspiration, and solid advice from a leader and mentor." - **Josh Mason**, USA, August 28, 2021

"**Important info!** - Dr. Hasib never fails to amaze me! I've learned so much from him both in college classes and outside. I've read both this book and his "Cybersecurity Leadership" book and feel confident in my abilities. The knowledge that he has shared has provided me with the strength to do well in job interviews and land my first one in a company with a great fit for me! Thank you so much Dr. Hasib, you never cease to amaze me!!" - **Allie White**, USA, September 2, 2021

"**Bring Inner Greatness Out** - ... words were inspirational. The book starts off with identifying personal branding, building relationships, and learning to express yourself confidently. It teaches valuable lessons that I think everyone should have the chance to learn. These lessons can be carried indefinitely throughout life as you interact with others personally and professionally..." Full review at: https://laureneason.com/2021/09/06/bring-inner-greatness-out/ - **Lauren Eason**, USA. September 6, 2021

"**A true guide for enabling your highest potential** - I have waited to give a review so I can cover the audio book several times and apply the information that is mentioned in the book. This book is narrated very well and Dr. Hasib has a very soothing voice. The information is relevant to all fields, but I had a better relation to his guidance because we are both in Cyber Security. I covered this book several times because I would listen to the parts that were relevant for a current situation, such as I would listen how to negotiate offers or opportunities while I was being contacted for jobs or events. Since listening to his book, I have made large leaps in my career. I have been able to transfer and promote internally to my company, I was a featured speaker for a Keynote event, and I am endlessly contacted for job offers. I have also helped other mentees grow as well. You may not grow in a day or week, but if you apply these principles you will grow in no time. I feel that Dr. Hasib has a wide range of knowledge and you can trust the information he provides. I also hold his other book in high regards, Cybersecurity Leadership, but I own the physical book not the audible book." - **Nicholas Scrima**, USA, September 9, 2021

CONTENTS

CHAPTER 1

Introduction

All of us are born unique and exceptional. Yet, too many of us spend a lifetime blending in and staying average. Society expects this from us. In pursuit of such mediocrity, we diminish our value and suppress the full monetary potential of our uniqueness and its accompanying greatness. We deny ourselves the happiness of living in our greatness. Choosing to embrace, refine, and flaunt our uniqueness and exceptionalism is far better. Living in our greatness is financially and emotionally more rewarding.

Our education system isn't helping either. Even though no two students are alike, our educational system does not try to uncover and refine the unique talents of each student. Instead, standardized teaching to dubious testing standards, reinforce mediocrity. We create additional testing and financial barriers for college admissions and perpetuate conditions that do not allow every student to get a fair chance.

Remarkably talented people are forced to feel inadequate in this system. Their individuality atrophies and they go through life without any chance of realizing their true potential. Instead of achieving greatness and living a life of fulfillment, they are cast aside as misfits. Even those who make it through, find themselves fighting a lifetime of uncertainty, and living on the edge of hunger and homelessness.

Imagine a piece of iron - worth a negligible amount of money. Would it make sense to simply wipe and clean it every now and keep it in that common state forever? Why not imagine all possible forms and shapes it could take? Imagine what happens when that piece of iron begins to refine, merges with other ingredients, and even suffers the blistering heat of a blacksmith's fire, or the sharp cuts of a manufacturing machine. It transforms into a far more valuable and useful state of existence. Even in its unfinished state, when it combines with the right ingredients, it becomes more valuable in the form of steel. You too can achieve such transcendence! Every human has this potential.

Do things because you can, not because you must. Continue to expand what you can do, and you will be amazed at your own prowess. This is the key to unlocking your value. Your expanding circles of people from various activities lead to more opportunities. Everyone is born knowing nothing; everything is learned. There is no end to human learning or growth.

Once distinction is achieved, you can flaunt this distinction and never refer to yourself as that original piece of iron even if society or hiring managers still look at you that way. *The accidental circumstances of our birth may create unique obstacles, but they never define our destiny.*

We must appreciate that no two people ever perform the same in any job! So, the idea of anyone earning the same as the last person in any job is absurd! It is also absurd to peg a job to an arbitrary budget number or even a pay band. Pay must be proportional to the value produced! This is the fundamental promise of capitalism!

Unfortunately, most people are unable to grasp or quantify their value. They are socialized into agreeing that it is okay for any company to maximize profits. Pay bands and budget based compensation have been normalized. People do not realize that companies are taking advantage of them by monopolizing power, stifling true competition, and denying them their right to enjoy the rewards of their labor and innovation.

It is time for value and profit producers to reclaim their power! That is the primary goal of this book - to empower you to find your greatness, refine it, quantify it, market it, promote it, flaunt it, and earn what you are truly entitled to earn. You know best what you can and cannot do. Your ability to do things is fluid and completely within your control.

You can choose to have more control over your life, or you can choose to live according to the wishes of others. You can choose to let others determine your worth or you can choose to define it yourself. You can choose to let others benefit from all the value and profits you create, or you can claim your fair share. You can choose to be yourself or fail in trying to be someone else. You can choose to be average or you can choose to be great!

Greatness is a choice. Greatness exists in all of us. You must search for it, find it, polish it, leverage it, package it, monetize it, and determine your success. This book shows you how. Go through this journey with me and you will never be average again! You will find that existing in your greatness is soul satisfying and a source of abundant happiness.

Living your purpose will bring you far more happiness than making extraordinary levels of money doing something you do not enjoy! Non-monetary rewards will give you higher and longer lasting value than monetary rewards. Living in your greatness will give you an unlimited supply of non-monetary rewards to go along with a comfortable flow of monetary rewards!

1.1 WHAT HAPPENED TO US?

During the last forty years, we have seen a steady decline in job security, retirement benefits, employee profit sharing, employee ownership, employee bargaining power, and healthcare benefits. We have seen a steady decline in real income, home ownership, access to higher education, and overall prosperity for most people.

Small businesses have been replaced with franchise powerhouses. Local culture and cuisine are vanishing. All cities are pockmarked by the same brands and signs. A small number of behemoth global corporations control job markets and the supply of goods and services. Real capitalistic competition has been replaced by monopoly and monopsony. The global pandemic of 2020 has exposed this harsh truth in more powerful ways than anything else could have.

Despite the enormous size of total profits generated from the value produced by working people, their ability to enjoy the benefits of their own labor and success has declined dramatically. Like all previous downturns, the economic recession of 2020 is likely to result in a larger redistribution of wealth to the wealthy. While producers of profits - the workers - go into bankruptcy and homelessness, a small number of oligarchs swallow up foreclosed homes and assets and concentrate even greater wealth into fewer hands.

Such concentration of power and income is justified as capitalism, and any effort to return the power to the individuals is mischaracterized and labeled as liberalism or socialism or even communism. Instead of worrying about simple labels, why not worry about what gives us better financial control over our own successes. Labels are usually used by people who wish to distract us into allowing them to perpetuate the status quo, which is overwhelmingly stacked against workers and value producers; the situation continues to worsen every day.

The fundamental promise of capitalism is individual success: If we work hard, we will enjoy the fruits of our hard work. In the past, this promise enabled true capitalistic economies to enjoy high levels of innovation, productivity, and individual wealth. Anyone doing anything productive enjoyed a decent living and could support their families.

Right now, a person's income is no longer proportional to their contribution to the profits and the value creation in an organization. Regardless of the profession anyone pursues, administrative people in positions of power disproportionately extract profits for themselves while leaving the producers of profits in a perpetual state of subsistence and uncertainty.

Money has taken over elections. Layoffs are commonplace and real power is not in the hands of value producers. Instead, they are in the hands of owners or executives hired by owners or boards. These disparities in power and income have permeated almost all types of organizations.

Top executives in organizations do not even need to have subject matter expertise in the verticals they run. People with generic MBA degrees find themselves in top executive positions with no prior experiences in retail, education, energy, or healthcare. People with PhDs in English and similar unrelated fields (even without terminal degrees) and no work experiences in complex new disciplines such as cybersecurity are appointed as Chief Academic Officers, Vice Provosts, Deans, and Chairs - frequently without competitive searches!

Too many top level people are hired because of who they know rather than what they know! When appointed, the first people they replace are the most qualified people for these jobs because they represent an existential threat to their own inadequacies. Sometimes, the most qualified people leave because they find it difficult to work for unqualified executives. Such travesty results in reduced revenue for the organization, lower quality service for everyone, and serious damage to the profession.

Executives in almost all organizations globally are using their power and authority to redistribute extraordinary proportions of profits and compensation to themselves. People who produce profits and value are so minimally compensated that they have difficulty affording basic food, clothing, shelter, and healthcare.

Since most executives lack expertise in the verticals they lead, they resort to simple budget manipulation, spreadsheets, and cost management techniques to manage all types of organizations. They use generic marketing and high pressure sales techniques to increase customers. They ignore investments in innovation and product quality. Instead, they protect market share by buying up competitors and by controlling supply through lobbying and funding politicians for favorable laws, regulations, and non-competitive allocation of contract work.

Free market capitalism has been diminished and antitrust protections have eroded. This distortion is glossed over by pundits as the natural outcome of capitalism. This phenomenon is the exact opposite of capitalism. True capitalism enables people to earn in accordance with their contributions and not in accordance with their positions of power and authority.

The result is economic apartheid. People with money use the power created through money to systematically prevent others from gaining money and associated power. They use financial power to redistribute more money to themselves by systematically funding elected policy makers who are financially beholden to them. In the meantime, the real producers of profits and value are scrambling to survive and teetering on the edge of homelessness and even death.

Whether we think of them in terms of gender, race, ethnicity, or sexual orientation, such economic apartheid has kept every marginalized group suppressed. Ethical considerations, which used to prevent such abuses of power, have largely disappeared. Lying and cheating by people in positions of power and authority are condoned because they have not expressly been made illegal.

We can debate the reasons why the decline happened, and we can try to use economic fairness arguments to make changes. We can organize, hold rallies, protests, sit ins, or million people marches. While these efforts may result in raising consciousness and make a few news headlines, at the end of the day, these efforts are largely ineffective - mainly because they rely on the actions of others.

Protests have not resulted in any real change in the balance of power or the equitable distribution of the fruits of capitalistic hard work and innovation. In fact, sometimes these efforts have resulted in further tyranny and even violent suppression by the people in positions of power and authority. In most cases, lip service and vague promises are used to placate people. However, since these executives lack integrity and their promises have no credibility, real change has not happened.

We can accept this as our fate; we can accept our disproportionate decline in income and power, or we can choose a different path: the path of our own greatness. Instead of focusing on macroeconomic issues or political problems that we have little chance of solving anytime soon, we can all focus on one thing that we have 100% control over - our own actions. *While we cannot control the actions of others, we have complete control over our own actions and reactions.*

We must realize that we are the producers of value and there is inherent power in the value we produce. Without the value we produce, no one can make profits! We need to think of ourselves as mini businesses and ourselves as the sole product. Just like a business, we need to develop as many customers and clients as possible; we need to create demand for the product.

If we are the product for our businesses and there is only one of us, imagine the possibilities and the power of monopoly pricing! That is what a compelling personal brand will give you. Every one of us needs to have a strong personal brand if we wish to profit from the value we produce! We can gain the power to determine our own income, job security, negotiating power, and overall prosperity and success.

A compelling personal brand will increase your professional worth and provide you with tangible, permanent, and ever increasing rates of return to your income stream. I invite you to take this journey with me. You must recognize that you are the value producer.

You produce value while working at home or outside the home. You produce value while cooking a meal, gardening, vacuuming the carpet, or even changing diapers. You produce value even if no one is paying you for it. Your goal should be to get paid for as much of this value as possible, from as many consumers as possible. This is how you can create multiple sources of income.

Without you, organizations cannot produce value. They hire you to produce value. Essentially, they are buying the value you produce. Unfortunately, they then give you a small share while retaining the bulk of the value for themselves; they are buying the value you produce at a rock bottom price. They use the power of monopsony in labor markets to pay you below market compensation. They act as though they are doing you a favor by giving you a job!

However, given the global marketplace of buyers for your goods and services, is there any reason for you to sell all your value production services to a single employer? Your main goal should be to make sure you realize the full value potential of all things you can do. Why sell only one service or a few services to one employer? Instead, you should be selling all your goods and services to multiple buyers or employers. This is already happening and is most likely the future of work.

Many current sources of power will disappear in the future world. What will not disappear is the human ability to produce value. Right now, banks use other people's money to make massive profits. Then they make poor loans and take on insane risks and then receive taxpayer bailouts because their demise will supposedly disrupt the economy. In true capitalism, unprofitable companies and executives should be replaced by profitable ones - not be propped up with the money from the very people they are exploiting.

Ask yourself why you should suffer the business losses of a failing company. If they were too big to fail in the first place, why are they even bigger now? Why is taxpayer money going to companies and not directly to the people? Instead of the government giving taxpayer money to companies to keep people hired, why not pay the people directly? Like doctors who must submit bills to insurance companies, why not make companies that keep employees on the payroll submit a bill to the government?

The American auto companies were "saved" by the taxpayers. So why didn't the taxpayers become owners of these companies? Why are we back in the same situation where these companies are losing money and laying off people? If you are bailing out a company, shouldn't you own the company as a cooperative? Shouldn't you be enjoying the profits from your investments in the bailed out company?

The main problem is that individuals have not gained full control of their sources of power yet. They have handed it over to others. They trust others to do the right thing. They are enabling others to profit from their work without receiving their own fair share. In the old economy, unions used to recoup some power for workers and value producers. Now, even that minimal power has largely vanished.

For decades, scholars have been giving away their works, doctoral dissertations, and other intellectual property to commercial databases who then resell access to these works to educational institutions, libraries, and sometimes even the scholars themselves! In the past, due to lack of mass communication technology, this may have been a necessary evil for the distribution of the work; right now, in the age of global connectivity, these arrangements make no sense.

In the new world, individuals can claim back their sources of power and even increase them by expanding their markets and economic might globally. In a hyperconnected global economy many new things are possible. Widespread adoption of new technologies such as blockchain may create a new type of economy within the next ten years.

Imagine a world where a taxi driver can charge the passenger directly for a ride without being forced to share anything with an intermediary who imparts minimal value, such as a semblance of trust, to the transaction. However, even that trust has often proved to be dubious. Thus, companies that own no cars and perform no work, other than providing some technology, can skim off massive profits from drivers who create the value.

What if the driver could control their own technology, or even lease it for a fee, and have a reputation of trust? Imagine a world where everyone is a mini clearinghouse of multiple services. Imagine a world where multiple individual entrepreneurs are collectively or cooperatively providing services directly to the buyers.

In such a world, the producers of value will get to keep most of the profits from the value they create. They will each become their own individual sources of power. Instead of meekly accepting a meager life being doled out to them by those in power, they would be able to focus on building richer lives using their own sources of power and influence fueled by compelling global personal brands. This book will guide you to such an empowering future.

1.2 WHY BUILD A PERSONAL BRAND?

Your personal brand will provide the following seven powerful benefits. These benefits are discussed in much greater detail later in the book.

WHY BUILD A PERSONAL BRAND?

Build Increased Value for Your Work
Help Market Your Ideas
Develop Confidence and Job Security
Gain Better Control of Your Career
Create Multiple Sources of Income
Increase Earnings
Personal Success Decoupled from Organization

Why Build a Personal Brand?

During the July 22, 2020 episode of Conversations With #DrCybersecurity, my dear friend for over two decades, Celeste Stacey, captured the essence of my message in this powerful statement, "People need to create their own economy. People need to take control of their income so they can control their outcome!" she said. This book will help you do exactly that: *Gain control of your income so you can determine your outcome!*

#DrCybersecurity

CHAPTER 2

Determining Your Compensation

Have you systematically calculated your market value? If a hiring manager asks you what you can do for their company, would you be able to quantify that in financial terms? If someone asks you how much compensation you desire, would you be able to discuss the financial value you will produce before answering the question? Do you realize that depending on the company, your ability to produce value will be different? Does it really make sense for you to ask for the same compensation at every company?

Do you have a sphere of influence? How large is your sphere? Is it global? What is the value of this sphere of influence? Will it result in more sales for any company you decide to affiliate with? Shouldn't this value be part of your compensation negotiations? If you do decide to make your sphere of influence part of the package for your hire, how will you ensure your contacts and sphere of influence remain yours and does not suddenly become co-opted by the company you decide to join?

What happens to future contacts? What about courses, programs, books, articles, videos, teaching tools, or anything you have authored and might adapt for use by your employer? While it might be okay for your employer to gain the right to use these adaptations, your own right to reuse them for other clients or employers should not be curtailed. Should you really be limiting your ability to earn a living from your own intellectual property?

You must think through these questions carefully and develop good answers for all these questions. Your answers should be easily validated by your digital public profile and record of accomplishments. If you do not have quantifiable and confident answers to these questions and do not have a strong digital profile of your accomplishments, you will be at a serious disadvantage during salary negotiations.

If the compensation offer is low, you will lack a strong basis for asking more. One key point you need to remember: Different people in the same position will produce different levels of value. So, smart organizations are usually willing to pay someone according to their value. However, they will not do so automatically.

The argument that everyone in the same job should be paid the same, is inherently flawed. Arguments that a woman should be paid the same as a man or that people of all races should make the same, may appear fair on the surface. However, these arguments have never gained traction because no two people ever produce the exact same value in any job. If a woman produces more value than any man or woman in a job, she should be making more - not equal to anyone else. Arguments based on value production are far more likely to succeed.

No two people are the same. Their backgrounds, education, skills, job experiences, and personal brands are not identical. The value of a person in any job is often determined by duties, skills, and qualifications that may be outside the job requirements. Therefore, they cannot be expected to produce equal value. Therefore, performance based pay, is usually the fairest form of compensation. Hence, performance based arguments are far more likely to yield better results.

Similarly, budget based pay bands created by finance officers, without taking market realities into account, do not make sense either. While these pay bands may look great on a spreadsheet and may make budgeting easier for executives, they are crutches and demonstrate a lack of understanding of proper value based hiring practices. They also reflect a failure to set market based pay. They certainly fail to appreciate the value people create.

These convenient pay bands were created for a different era when humans were viewed as simple labor and their value was determined by how many items they could produce or assemble in an assembly line. In a knowledge economy, these pay bands are anachronistic. Technology and human innovation allow a single human to produce items with a wide range of values. For example, a professor can teach but that professor can also recruit many students and promote the university in a dramatic way. Should they only be paid for teaching? If so, should they stop doing all the other activities?

As finance officers took over the reins of companies during the last forty years, companies have been increasingly using these artificial pay structures and prenegotiated compensation as a precondition before a candidate is even referred to the hiring manager. While these practices are convenient for the exceptionally well paid executives, they represent a failure of these executives to understand the modern economy and the value of humans in a knowledge economy; these practices guarantee that the wrong candidate will be hired most of the time. They also cause jobs to remain unfilled for prolonged periods of time. Organizations and executives use convenient excuses such as "skills gap" to explain keeping critical positions vacant.

Some of the best qualified candidates will not agree to a salary figure before assessing the work involved, benefits, and the overall value of the position against their own personal goals and career trajectory. Most will also want to get a sense of their supervisors and team members. Furthermore, no real salary negotiations can happen until a strong candidate has been able to properly express the financial value they will produce; they must gain an understanding of the value creation opportunities in each prospective role.

I always refused to pre-negotiate compensation before the interview. While this resulted in not being interviewed for several jobs, I felt it was also a good way to screen out companies and hiring managers I should not be working for. Any company that was unwilling to rethink such an unreasonable practice was far more budget-focused and not focused enough on hiring the right employee. We should not enable these unreasonable practices!

In one instance, the HR person lied to the hiring manager that my asking salary was too high even though I had not shared any number; I had simply stated, "I will not negotiate salary until a job offer has been made." The hiring manager called me to verify and we were both surprised by the misrepresentation. I was interviewed and an offer well below market was made. I proposed an acceptable compensation, which the hiring manager also agreed was reasonable, but was overruled by the Chief Financial Officer.

Working for such companies would never make sense for me since they would never appreciate my value afterwards either! I also found that organizations that relaxed this practice of pre negotiating salaries to interview me, eventually ended up offering more that their initial pay range once they recognized the value, I was bringing in.

Organizations must appreciate that every job has a value and a cost. Every candidate will evaluate if the value of the job is higher than the personal cost and sacrifice that the candidate will need to make in the job. Even travel, moving, and commuting costs could impact the value proposition of a job. If the value of the job is not higher than the personal cost, candidates will not accept jobs or even interview for them.

Since different people have different abilities to produce value, compensation must be tied to this level of value. An employee who produces $1,000,000 value per year and wants to be paid $200,000 is a far better hire than another employee who is willing to accept $100,000 but will only produce $200,000 in value every year!

Similarly, if a particular woman can produce far more value than any man or woman in the same job, she should be asking for a higher salary than men - not equal! The women's world soccer team is a great example where women were framing the argument around gender equality instead of framing their argument on revenue and success. If they asked to be paid in proportion to the value and revenue they generated, their arguments would have been more powerful.

Job applicants, with no understanding of their market value and no demonstrable representation of the value they will bring to a position, are at a serious disadvantage. They will be forced to accept whatever an organization offers them - most often based on what the previous person may have made. Sometimes they will offer to start a worker at the bottom of the scale for a particular position - invariably with the promise that longevity will allow compensation to grow - something that invariably will not happen. Initial low pay may stifle future progress within a company forever.

2.1 VALUE VS PRICE

Why do we buy anything? To answer this question, we must delve into the psychology of sales. We buy something when we perceive its value to be higher than the price. This psychology of buying is powerful. The higher our perceived value versus the price, the more likely we are to buy something. Whatever your chosen profession, you must internalize this basic principle of selling anything.

We are chemical beings and much of our activities and decisions are controlled by the chemicals released by our brains. When we see a bargain, our brain releases powerful chemicals encouraging a purchase. Therefore, Black Friday sales can draw massive lines and even become violent as we compete for a bargain. This is also why we frequently buy things we do not need at a flea market or a garage sale. When something is free, we all want it; the perceived value can be compulsively high. This leads to impulsive purchases of things we do not need.

Perception of value is also uniquely individual. Therefore, the same product can be sold at different prices to different people. While some of us may buy a particular shirt for $10, others may be willing to buy it at $15 or even $20. Every buyer can still be happy with their purchase if their perceived value is higher than the price. This is also why everyone loves to brag about a bargain.

This is the simple economics of buying. Even if we buy a bottle of water, we always make the same evaluation: Is the value higher than the price? Merchants know this well. Therefore, to them, selling anything at the same price to everyone makes no sense.

To maximize profits, merchants resort to tiered pricing. They price something at a high price for a few days or weeks ensuring that they can make higher profits from buyers willing to pay those higher prices. Later they lower prices to sell to buyers at the lower price ranges.

Merchants also use various marketing strategies such as discount signs, sales, and two for one schemes - all designed to increase our perception of value. Even staging and displays in the store can dramatically affect our perception of value for anything. There is no monetary difference between buying two pairs of shoes at $40 per pair or $80 total. Yet, when we enter a shoe store with a two for one sale, we invariably assign a higher perceived value on every pair of shoes. We end up buying two pairs even if we may need one.

Our perceived value of the same item can also change dramatically based on supply and circumstances. Under ordinary circumstances we may be willing to pay 25 cents for a bottle of water. However, at an airport, after we have gone through the security checkpoint, our willingness to pay $2 or ever higher for that same bottle of water increases dramatically.

If there is a limited supply of anything, our perception of value for that item rises. Thus, a rare coin or a single painting by an artist can be sold at exceptionally high prices. Due to the increased value of their works, the personal brand value of most artists also rises after death. Suppliers work hard to restrict availability of products, often by restricting complete information, to sustain higher prices.

We need to think of ourselves in the same manner - after all there is only one of us in the entire world! About time we capitalized on this undeniable fact!

2.2 MAKING THE SALE - AT A HIGHER PRICE

Given this human phenomenon of value vs price judgements, logically there are two ways to make all sales:

1. Reduce price to make value appear higher than the price, or
2. Increase value to make price appear lower than value.

Option one reduces profits. However, option two has tremendous promise for increased profits. If we can increase the perceived value of something high enough, we can surely increase its price - resulting in even higher profits for us. This is exactly what good sales agents do. This is also how two parties typically bargain during price negotiations.

In the area of real estate sales, high quality real estate agents work to ensure that the property they are representing shows well. Appearance of a property can dramatically impact the perceived value in the minds of buyers as well as appraisers. Even paint, wallpaper, and cleanliness can impact the perceived value of a property significantly.

During my ten years as a real estate agent, I had the opportunity to refine and execute this key sales principle, which resulted in successful sales at higher prices for properties I represented and sold. Since my compensation was based on the sale price of the home, the higher the selling price, the higher was my commission.

Everything started with the initial listing presentation. First, I dressed professionally to exude competence. Then, I delivered a unique presentation showcasing original thinking, knowledge, market analysis, and expertise. My years of training and practice as a public speaker worked in my favor as I delivered a smooth unfaltering presentation containing the following key elements:

1. Market research along with a statistical projection on the number of sales likely in the neighborhood within the next 90 days. This would give us a sense of the supply and demand ratio and allow my client to select the listing price appropriately. For example, if only two sales were likely, then an aggressive price in a downward moving market may result in no sale at all for my client.
2. Explanation that the best way to obtain the highest possible price is to ensure that the property is exposed to 100% of the market;

based on my experience and analysis this takes roughly three weeks.

3. Explanation that a bidding war on the first day usually means the property has been priced too low; these bidding wars should never be the goal because it usually results in a quick sale for the agent but a lower price for the seller.

4. Explanation that people will buy for a higher price if we can increase the perceived value of the home.

5. Provision of a one year warranty on the home through a warranty company, which would invariably increase the perceived value of the property for any buyer.

6. Explanation of how brokerage commissions work and why they needed to be generous with commissions. I explained that the cost of the commission is built into the price of the home anyway. This is like the marketing costs of any product being built into the price of the product, which is always paid by the buyer!

7. Explanation that discount agents invariably end up exposing the property to a much smaller slice of the market resulting in a lower price.

8. Explanation that my sales model suggested that the seller pay a slightly higher commission for a buyer's agent compared to other sellers. This would mean that the buyer's agent would have a higher incentive to show their property. This would increase market exposure. In addition, being the first home to be shown to a buyer might make it far more likely to be sold at a higher price. This strategy invariably meant that even if there would be one sale in the neighborhood that season, it would be my client's property. In a falling market, this strategy protected my sellers from thousands of dollars in losses.

9. Explanation of how For Sale by Owner worked and why they generally resulted in a much lower price for the seller; the property gets exposed to a much smaller segment of the market and buyers invariably try to bargain the seller down even further.

10. Explanation that as part of my staging strategy for the property, we would need to power wash the house, shampoo the carpet, reduce clutter and extra furniture, and even do some minor repairs such as fix holes in walls, repair damage to vinyl floors, and replace oxidized window panes with broken seals (as these might have to be replaced anyway due to a home inspection).

11. Explanation that as part of my marketing strategy, I would prepare well worded descriptions of the property designed to evoke emotions and inspire a buyer's imagination. I would take lots of photographs, create color flyers, put up a professional looking high quality sign, and even do short distance radio broadcasts describing the property so buyers would be able to listen to a human voice describing the property from their car radios as they drove near the property.

12. Finally, a promise that I would be the best real estate agent they would ever experience in their life. To prove this, I would share the written results of all the client surveys and the comments from the clients. My goal was to get ten out of ten in every category of service listed in the survey. In ten years of working as a real estate agent, I never received less than ten out of ten in any category. In most cases, my clients rated above the scale!

This sales strategy allowed me to compete based on value rather than price and allowed me to earn higher compensation; I also gained a deeper understanding of marketing to people. I also noted with great interest the incredible power of successful agents over their brokers. All individual workers who produce value need to gain similar power.

2.3 PACKAGING OURSELVES FOR BEST VALUE

Now that you understand how sales work and how value must be increased to obtain a higher price, imagine your personal brand and your services as products you wish to sell at the highest price possible. You must compete on value and not on price. Your total value includes all aspects of your being. Most job candidates fail to bring all of themselves to a job interview. Most people do not apply all of themselves to a job either.

All jobs have two components: 1) the defined roles that the manager and the organization expect and 2) the undefined roles that can be added simply because of the skills, talents, interests, and passion of the person occupying the role. If the defined role is being performed as expected, the undefined roles can be a major source of growth, learning, satisfaction, and even extra income and promotional opportunities.

Most people have never consciously worked to bring out their inner greatness. Nor have they consciously developed their personal brand and projected the value of this personal brand to the market. Hence, during a job interview, they fail to show their inner greatness or their wide range of talents - many of which might be outside the requirements listed in the job description.

To illustrate this point, let me share this story about how I got hired for a full-time job as an English teacher at an international elementary school after finishing high school. My English professor knew the principal of an elementary school who was looking for an English teacher. So, he took me on his motorbike to meet with the principal.

I was seventeen with long curly hair and Elvis Presley sideburns. It was the cool look of the 1970s. However, my hair and sideburns reduced my perceived value in the eyes of the principal, and she rejected me right away! My professor persisted and offered the following statement: "But sister, he has many other talents. He can sing and play the guitar!"

Suddenly, the perceived value of my services as an English teacher went up! The principal turned to me and asked, "Can you teach young children to sing and to play the guitar?"

"Sister I have never done this before, but I am willing to try," I said - clinching the job offer! The key is to bring as much of ourselves as possible to a job interview.

The value perception we reflect starts with our resume and cover letter and continues all the way to our digital presence, published works, public recommendations on LinkedIn and other forums, videos, interviews, personal grooming, the credibility of our references, and a wide range of things that make our inner greatness come out and make our personal brand shine.

Our preparation for the job interview is critical. If we research all members of the interview team, we may find ways to create a connection. For example, if a committee member has won an award, a candidate might create an instant bond by congratulating the person sometime during the interview. If the company has won an award, why not congratulate everyone on the accomplishment at the beginning of your interview? These little gestures will set you apart.

Before a hiring manager or a company makes a hiring decision, they make the same simple calculation that every buyer makes: Does the value of the individual exceed the price? If so, by how much? How does it compare with the other choices? Will we enjoy working around this person? Will this person be helpful to others, and will this person be willing to learn from others?

In other words, which hire will produce the highest value for the organization in exchange for the compensation they are paid? A candidate's communications, interpersonal skills, and ability to create a connection will increase their perceived value. No hiring manager will ever hire a person if they evaluate value to be lower than the price. Our goal should be to ensure that the perception of our value is as high as possible to a hiring manager. Reducing the salary, we are willing to accept, will never work in our favor!

Even though these are usually illegal, personal biases such as gender, race, or even national origin can impact a hiring manager's perception of value. Cultural biases play into these perceptions of value as well. Due to such biases, hiring managers are often willing to pay more for employees of a particular gender or race.

How can we effectively counter such compensation biases? While there are discrimination laws protecting us from job opportunity biases, there are no laws protecting us from job compensation biases. Both types of biases are difficult to prove and may not be worth the personal and financial toll to pursue. Your best defense and offense against such biases is the value of your personal brand! You will find that the strength of your personal brand will often transcend gender, race, or ethnic biases!

2.4 PAY ACCORDING TO REVENUE VS PAY ACCORDING TO AUTHORITY

Ever wonder why movie stars or TV personalities - specially those at the top of their profession - make so much more money? Why do football or baseball players make so much? Why do their coaches or managers make far less money than the players?

In the corporate world, we cannot imagine our bosses ever making less than us. Within the hierarchy of a typical organization, pay is determined by position, rank, and level of authority rather than actual production of value. This pay discrepancy has exacerbated during the last forty years. Hence, a typical CEO (the ultimate in power and authority in an organization) today receives about four hundred times more than the average worker; about forty years ago their compensation was roughly forty times an average worker's compensation.

Yet, like baseball players, workers who produce the highest levels of value in any organization are usually far lower down in the organization. The primary difference is that movie stars, TV personalities, and sports stars have strong personal brands. Even the mere association of a strong personal brand with a product completely unrelated to their area of expertise, will enhance the perceived value of that product.

By enhancing value, they can generate more sales of the product. Thus, a successful athlete or a movie star can be featured in an ad for breakfast cereal and immediately increase sales of the product. In other words, since the personal brands of these stars enhance the value of a corporate brand or product, they can earn compensation proportional to their contribution.

Affiliation with these individuals imparts value to any organization or product; and these individuals can connect their compensation to the value they create. They negotiate based on the value they create; they quantify the value and use it as leverage during contract negotiations. Therefore, the same position players on different teams make different levels of compensation.

Why does this happen? To reinforce this, we must appreciate that the value of anything is dramatically fluid. Value fluctuates widely based on time and circumstances. Value is simply what someone perceives it to be. Sales and marketing professionals know this principle and their entire effort in making a sale is focused on increasing the perceived value of any product through conversation, demonstration, complimentary add-ons, and other marketing tools. Their goal is never to reduce the price to increase the perceived value.

Understanding your value is the most critical first step in negotiating your compensation. As you increase your value through the development of your personal brand, you will be able to command higher levels of compensation. You will also be able to develop multiple streams of income, which will help you lower the risks of any single income stream.

During my ten years as a licensed real estate agent, I noticed that successful real estate agents were particularly good at developing a valuable personal brand. They farmed certain neighborhoods and achieved name recognition and personal brand value that far exceeded the name recognition and brand value of the companies they were affiliated with. This translated into more business for them.

In most cases, people could name the agent but could not name the company. Agents could move from company to company without any loss of business income. Their clients moved with them. These agents were highly effective in tying their own compensation to their production of value.

Agents without brand name recognition could not compete. Therefore initially, when I had no sales history, I had to compete on an innovative market analysis and an innovative sales presentation and marketing strategy! Without a unique, confident, and unfaltering presentation, which would show my value as a high quality agent, I stood no chance!

Most real estate agents are not employees. Instead, they share a portion of their earnings with the company or broker they affiliate with.

The income of the broker and the brokerage firm is therefore 100% dependent on the hiring and retention of successful real estate agents.

New real estate agents usually must give up 50% or more of their commission earnings to the broker, while experienced successful agents can negotiate retaining 80% or more of their commissions! What if all of us could keep 80% or more of the value we produce through our work? After all, isn't the income and profits of any organization 100% dependent on our work and the value we produce?

In the case of teachers and professors this fact is most clear. Students pay for education as a product, which is produced and delivered by the teachers and professors. Certainly, just like baseball organizations, there are overhead costs for any school or university. However, the value produced by a teacher or professor can easily be calculated by the number of students the teacher or professor attracts.

So why shouldn't teachers and professors expect their pay to be proportional to their contribution? Why shouldn't it be connected to the number of students they are teaching? Why shouldn't anyone in any field expect to be paid proportional to their contribution?

2.5 HAS IT ALWAYS BEEN THIS WAY?

Organizational hiring wasn't always this way. Companies used to recognize that different people represent different levels of value and negotiated in good faith with the employees they wanted. Therefore, companies used to compete to hire more valuable employees with perks such as healthcare, paid vacations, sick leave, retirement benefits, regular promotions, education benefits, and other similar offerings.

Such value based hiring still happens at the top executive levels. However, at lower levels, organizations have used a wide range of schemes and contracts to systematically eliminate competition in labor markets to gain leverage in compensation, remove perks, and reduce job security. Even knowledge workers and highly skilled workers are treated like assembly line workers producing widgets and their differences in value production are completely ignored during salary negotiations.

Compensation for mid and lower level workers have lost their connection to value production to such an extent that typical workers cannot even save enough to tide them over when they are laid off. Such lack of savings also prevents them from walking away from job situations where they are forced by employers to do illegal or unethical acts.

Layoffs are used to balance budgets and to increase profits. In most cases, such layoffs save the jobs of the executives but invariably hurt the organization because the people who are laid off are the main value creators. However, this fact is lost because the outdated accounting systems used by organizations treat people as expenses and never keep track of the value each worker produces! On top of that there is a lag in the revenue loss to be felt by the organization.

Thus, in the short term, a layoff appears to save money by reducing expenses because the lost revenue that the employees were bringing in or producing are never accounted for right away. The fact that most layoffs are a symptom of executive failure to manage risks and budget is glossed over. People have lost even the minimal power of job security they used to have.

Even government jobs, where job security was used to offset low pay, are no longer secure. We have a precarious situation where organizational executives have dramatically increased their control over our incomes through the systematic use of organizational power. Thus, most people have lost their ability to determine their destiny and to lead happy, healthy, and prosperous lives. The only way out of this terrible situation is for us to recognize and develop alternative sources of power and then leverage these sources of power to gain better control over our incomes and outcomes.

There are three key new sources of power - completely independent of the organizations we work for that we must recognize, embrace, and monetize: Knowledge, network, and personal brand. However, all three are consolidated within our personal brand. Bringing out our inner greatness and developing a compelling personal brand will provide us with an almost unlimited source of power!

As more people embrace this vital reality, and empowered people band together, create multiple sources of income, and collaboratively choose not to work for organizations unless compensation is tied to contribution, the balance of power in salary negotiations will start to change. Congratulations on your journey to your greatness!

CHAPTER 3

What is a Personal Brand?

Personal brands are like corporate brands; they convey a message to members of the public. We have seen strong corporate brands such as Google become verbs; some such as Kleenex or Xerox even replaced common nouns such as facial tissue or photostat! Such positive brand name recognition usually translates into higher brand value and profits. Corporate brands can also suffer from notoriety, which can result in reduction of brand value and profits. Personal brand value works the same way.

Our personal brand conveys our passion. It usually starts with our name and the way our name is displayed. Our name can be adorned with certifications or salutations such as Dr. or CISSP, PMP, CPHIMS. Such adornments usually add value. The more recognizable these adornments, the larger their impact; they speak on our behalf without us needing to do so. Nonverbal communications are powerful.

The way we dress, behave, and talk is also associated with our personal brand. Sometimes we may embrace a symbol to represent our personal brand. Such symbols can add intrigue, interest, and value to our brand. They can also generate questions and initiate conversations!

Our personal brand should reflect our values and the causes we support. Most importantly, our personal brand must stand on its own and be independent of any organizational brand. When people search for words associated with our passion, our work should be prominently displayed in the results.

For example, for my personal brand as Cybersecurity Leader, when people search for these words, my name and work should show up prominently in the search results. The higher we show up in the search results, the more success we have achieved in establishing our personal brand. As shown in the picture below, a personal brand has several key elements.

WHAT IS A PERSONAL BRAND?

**What You Stand For
The Way Your Name is Displayed
Your Values
The Symbols You Embrace
Your Mission in Life
The Causes You Support
What Your Actions, Words, and Deeds Convey
Independent of Any Organizational Brand**

What is a Personal Brand?

3.1 WHAT YOU STAND FOR

What issues do you most care about? What things do you hold so dear that you would never accept a job where you cannot get some of those things? What are some things worth more to you than any amount of money? Would you work for an unethical manager? Would you work for an unethical company? Would you be willing to lie?

Take a few minutes and write down some responses to these questions and other similar questions. Create a list of non-negotiable items. Maintain a separate list of additional things you desire that will help you decide between job offers. If any of the non-negotiable needs are unmet, you would automatically reject the job; perhaps you would not even apply.

Additional desired items in your list will help you weigh different job offers; they will even help you differentiate between the value of job offers. As you define what you stand for, the foundation of your personal brand will begin to form.

3.2 THE WAY YOUR NAME IS DISPLAYED

Next, think of your name. This is the most important decision. By what name do you want to be known? In what name would you like to be famous? Do you have a preferred way you like to be called? If so, do you display your name in all public settings in that preferred manner?

Take a few minutes to write down your answers to all these questions. Your name is your personal brand! So, choose carefully. Ideally, be prepared never to change this name; every time you change the name, the brand value will change - up or down.

Carefully choose the exact spelling and the way you always want your name to be displayed. Then, make sure that is the way you are listed in all public forums. Your legal name and the name you prefer to use are not always the same! Think of your personal brand as your global stage name. Inconsistency with your name will create personal brand dilution.

If you prefer to be called something but your name displays something else, once again you will have brand dilution. If your name has multiple words, consider if simplifying your name might give you better brand recognition. Sometimes, the complicated name or an interesting spelling or capitalizations of certain letters may create additional brand distinction. This is not an easy decision. So, choose carefully.

You also need to weigh the brand value advantages and disadvantages of changing your name every time your marital status changes. Always remember that every time your name appears in any forum, your personal brand is promoted. Therefore, after years of brand value and goodwill creation, changing your name may or may not be in your best interest. When your name is searched for, your entire body of work should surround you. If your name changes, some of your work will not show up in searches.

3.3 YOUR VALUES

What values do you hold dear? What values define you? What values shape your behavior? Our behavior is shaped by our values. If integrity is one of your core values, then you are unlikely to lie. If integrity is one of your core values, you are unlikely to enjoy working for an unethical employer or an unethical boss. Take a few minutes to write down three to six values that guide your behavior.

As you begin to strengthen and project your personal brand, everyone who comes across you should become aware of your values through your words, actions, and deeds. You will find that you associate better with people who align with your core values. You will also thrive and be happier in organizations that share your core values. You will have difficulty working with people and organizations with incongruent values. Values define the culture of organizations.

3.4 THE SYMBOLS YOU EMBRACE

Is there a symbol that could represent your brand? Just as an organization can have a brand symbol, your personal brand can be represented by symbols, objects, pictures, or even logos. Choose symbols that will generate curiosity and questions without words being spoken. Choose symbols that will allow you to share a story explaining the deeper meaning behind your chosen symbol and why that symbol represents your personal brand.

People will remember the story and that will help them affiliate strongly with your personal brand. If they really like your story, they might retell your story - further reinforcing your personal brand in their own minds as well as in the minds of others. Carefully selected symbols and brand logos silently inspire curiosity and questions. Such curiosity and questions lead to conversations; conversations are the beginnings of relationships with people. More relationships with more people will create more business opportunities for you and will be powerful contributors to the strength of your personal brand.

While talking about personal branding at a conference, I met someone who told me he calls himself the Kevin Bacon of the cybersecurity field. I suggested he use a couple of bacon pieces as the logo for his business card. A few weeks later, he reached out to tell me how stunned he was by the number of conversations his new business card initiated.

In my case, the picture of the crested giant saguaro has not only generated hundreds of conversations, it has resulted in promoting my books, my work, and my personal brand -- all without any words being spoken!

3.5 YOUR MISSION IN LIFE

Do you have a life purpose? What do you want your legacy to be? What would you like to be remembered for? What do you want your followers, supporters, and friends to celebrate you for? What type of job will allow you to fulfill your life purpose? Take a few moments to write down your answers to these questions. If you do not have good answers to these questions or have never thought about them that is fine for now.

However, now that you are going through this book, think about these questions and write down your answers; these answers will help you find and focus on your life goals. Such life goals are critical for establishing your personal brand; they are critical in helping you decide your personal mission and what you will and will not do. Actions in harmony with your life goals will usually be inspiring and meaningful to you, while other activities may feel like drudgery.

You will find that when you work towards your mission in life, you will be driven. Your work will not feel like work. You will be so engrossed in your passion that you will not feel tired. Every little achievement will inspire you some more. You will constantly have good feeling chemicals flowing throughout your body!

When your work is your passion and fulfills the mission of your life, you are more likely to bring all of yourself to the work. The more aspects of your being you can bring to the job, the more value you will produce and the happier you will be. You will also redefine the job in your own personally branded image making it impossible for someone else to do the same job and produce the same level of value. The value of your personal brand will impart so much value to the role that separation will hurt the organization far more than it will ever hurt you!

When your personal brand imparts significant value to an organization and a job role, you will become the face of the organization in that aspect. Since your personal brand imparts credibility to an organization, any separation will reduce the organization's credibility and value and the organization will immediately lose clients. In most cases, clients will follow you because they associate the service and the value they receive from the service with you. People bond with people, not with organizations. This is how you must perform in every role.

Instead, if your work is just a job and not a calling, you may find yourself unmotivated. If your job is incongruent with your values and not in support of your mission in life, and you are simply doing it to make a living, you will be under a constant state of stress with bad chemicals flowing throughout your body. This can even create health issues and cause your brain to function at a far lesser capacity than it is capable of.

If your boss or coworkers are oppressive or unsupportive, your stress level is likely to be even higher. In addition, due to the constant stress, you will be in a perpetual amygdala hijack condition and your brain will operate in a dramatically reduced capacity.

3.6 THE CAUSES YOU SUPPORT

When you pursue a primary mission in life, you will find yourself supporting several causes that support your mission. You may also find yourself supporting various causes that are not focused on your primary mission. You will support some causes due to your family members or friends. Take some time to list all the causes you support.

After you have written them all down, ask yourself if each cause you support are in harmony with each other and your primary mission in life or are they incongruous with your primary mission. For example, suppose you are a restaurant owner or a businessperson. Your primary mission is serving all your customers. Do you really want to take sides in politics or religion also?

Would it make business sense to divide your customers? If you are a singer or an actor, do you really wish to reduce your audience by taking sides in politics or religion? In general, any peripheral causes you support that might detract from your primary mission should be evaluated very carefully. Make a conscious choice and a cost benefit calculation for every cause you support.

3.7 WHAT YOUR ACTIONS, WORDS, AND DEEDS CONVEY

What are some common phrases you use? What are some common activities you engage in? Which types of activities are you most likely to participate in and which types would you typically avoid? In what forums do you express your words, actions, and deeds? Make a list of these.

Your words, actions, and deeds reveal aspects of your personal brand. They can support your mission if you are conscious about them. They can also detract from your mission if you are not careful about them. Your personal brand is reflected in every forum you participate in.

In an electronic era, with the perpetual existence of our digital footprints, every action in the digital world matters. Tweets, Retweets, Likes, Shares, Comments, Posts, and replies all matter. The impact of these actions can last a long time and can be relevant before, during, and after a job interview. They can also be relevant after you are hired.

While a social media rant and name calling in a fit of anger may feel good, the ultimate impact is likely to be more negative than positive.

You will always be much better off staying professional in your digital life. Chats, texts, emails, can come back to haunt you. Your digital footprint could even prevent you from gaining security clearances. The sooner you gain control of your words, actions, and deeds, and channel them to support your mission in life, the more successful you will be.

3.8 INDEPENDENT OF ANY ORGANIZATIONAL BRAND

Finally, your personal brand must stand on its own. Such independence is the most important attribute of your personal brand! Your personal brand should not be tied to a role in an organization and must be separate and distinct from the organizational brand. Your personal brand should provide the sheen on the organizational brand! It is the packaging that sells the organization; remove the packaging and the organization shines a lot less!

You must be in command of the relationship such that you impart far more value to your job and organization than it imparts to you. You should be the reason people are drawn to the organizational brand!

Such subservience of any organizational brand must be clear in all your personal brand projection activities. Always remember, people create the reputation for any organization.

Do not blindly assume that organizational branding is solely the responsibility of the Marketing department. Every person associated with a company in any way, is a brand representative. You may be in a better position than the Marketing department to promote the program or initiative you are associated with. Your clients will not develop relationships with the Marketing department; they will build these long-term relationships with you!

Separation from your job must not diminish the brand promotional activities you engage in. The public should continue to interact with you in the same manner as before and your clientele should stay aligned with you. Get competent legal advice and examine contract clauses related to clients; your clients and sphere of influence should remain yours. If you brought clients and employees in, they should be free to follow you. People affiliate with people - not organizations. Guard your connections and protect their privacy; no one should be soliciting your connections!

Be very wary of organizational efforts to co-opt your sphere of influence and connections - specially those that you accumulated before affiliating with any company. Your connections and clientele might be your intellectual assets and an integral part of your ability to earn a living. Get competent legal advice on these issues - specially if you are dealing with a corporate lawyer who is representing an organization. A corporate lawyer's job is to represent the interests of the company - not you!

From your clientele's perspective, your departure will diminish the credibility and value of the organizational brand! If the organization laid you off, the financial loss to the organization will be even more acute and rapid because your network will typically warn their networks not to expect the same high quality of service. The negative news will reverberate through people networks at lightning speed; bad news travels faster than good news!

Once you can establish a relationship where your personal brand increases the value of an organizational brand and your departure results in a significant loss of revenue for the organization, you may be able to engineer a grand return with more power and authority. The separation and reunification of Steve Jobs and Apple is one prominent example of this type of phenomenon.

I recognized these brand value principles and methodology in my own personal experiences every time I attached my personal brand to any initiative. It could be a conference, a program, or even an organization. The perception of value for the initiative increased every time I lent my personal brand to the effort. This is what you must strive to achieve.

When I taught for a university, students joined the program simply to study under my care. Their primary reasons were credibility, competence, and trust. My personal brand association with academic cybersecurity programs and my professional activities lent a dramatically high level of credibility to these programs and brought in thousands of students to all cybersecurity programs without any marketing expenses.

My speaking activities and earned media marketing helped enrollment in all programs just like a rising tide lifts all boats. My appearances on TV, conference keynotes, writings, interviews, individual and program awards, my conversations with current and prospective students, my mentoring, and the success of my students and graduates dramatically increased the global reputation and enrollment in all university programs I was associated with - all without any marketing expenses!

Students, graduates, and their parents who had experienced the high quality education automatically became ambassadors of the programs. This word of mouth continued to bring in an increasingly steady stream of thousands of students. Many were excited to tell me they joined because of a video, TV interview, or a recommendation from a trusted friend or supervisor.

When I talked with prospective students at enrollment drives or webinars, we also had a high conversion rate. When many others and I departed due to a mass layoff, there was a dramatic decline in enrollment. There was a significant loss of free earned media. Instead of saving money for the university, the layoff resulted in a precipitous decline in revenue, quality, and reputation.

The students noted the change in quality of service immediately and complained vigorously both in person and in social media, which resulted in an even larger decline in revenue and reputation. Of course, the faculty also noted the leadership vacuum, reduced quality of support, delays in fixing problems and errors, and delays in critical updates to the classroom materials, which directly impacted their own ability to teach and support students effectively; they too stopped championing the programs.

Since I had redefined my position in accordance with my unique self, it became impossible for anyone to fill the position without the clients and the organization sensing the vacuum! When I joined a new university, hundreds of students followed. Overall interest in the entire new university increased because people learned of the university and its programs through my marketing and brand promotion activities.

I had requested the enrollment personnel of the new university to keep track of increased traffic and they confirmed that they clearly saw a sharp increase in applications and interest in all cybersecurity and related programs at the new university, the timing of the increase coincided exactly with the start of my promotional activities. That is the power of an independent personal brand!

3.8.1 Inoculating Against Layoffs

In an era of perpetual layoffs, failure to build an independent personal brand will leave you highly vulnerable to the financial risks of a layoff. In such cases, your brand and market value will reduce dramatically whenever you separate from an organization. Once your brand value is diminished, you will have a hard time getting new opportunities.

This is exactly why it is harder for people to find a job when they are unemployed. If long periods of unemployment mean long periods of inactivity promoting and projecting your personal brand, then your personal brand will suffer an even larger decline in value. *Therefore, your personal brand enhancement related activities must never cease. Your professional activities must be independent of job roles.*

If your identity is tied to an organizational role, you may feel embarrassed to talk about a layoff; you might even worry that others will blame you and your future job prospects will diminish. Do not ever allow an organizational role to be the packaging around your personal brand! A layoff is not about you; instead, it reveals serious financial and executive leadership problems within the organization.

In the USA, you should consider having a consulting company registered in your name with a registered Federal Employer Identification Number with a 9-digit number assigned by the Internal Revenue Service. Your public speaking, consulting, and various other activities could always be done in the name of your company without having to reveal your Social Security Number to lots of people and companies. Your company and its accomplishments will also look good on your resume and provide a positive way to explain any gaps in your primary employment role in any organization.

Your professional activities after the layoff are extremely important. Researching companies, documenting your learning and results, speaking at events, taking free or paid training, volunteer activities, building lab or research environments, writing articles and books, making educational videos, and even helping others while you are networking for your next opportunity are all possible projects that will look helpful on your resume.

Your best defense is to be factual and open. Provide links to any publicly available stories. Give anyone who asks facts; facts without embellishment will work in your favor. Instead, if you try to hide or gloss over the layoff, you may hurt yourself with prospective employers.

Never denigrate any previous organization, organizational leader, or a previous supervisor. This is another reason why publicly available information is the best way to provide information. In most cases, you will never know the exact reason why organizational executives conducted a layoff.

In most cases, executives conduct mass layoffs because on the surface it appears fair. They can rationalize an across the board layoff of a certain percentage of people much better than targeted or strategic layoffs, which require more analysis and thinking. However, these types of indiscriminate layoffs always result in higher long term revenue loss compared to short term salary savings.

This is another reason why you should not attempt to provide reasons; tell anyone who asks you that you really do not know the exact reasons. Do not speculate on the reasons; there is usually a wide gap between public messaging and the actual truth. Facts and publicly available information will remove your emotions from the situation, and it will also help you heal faster from any loss of self-esteem. *You need to gain control over the layoff and not let the layoff control you!*

3.8.2 Celebrating Your Availability

Once you have established a strong personal brand and people can see plenty of evidence of your greatness, your availability in the job market should be viewed by others as a major opportunity to enhance the value of their organizational brands; they should be seeking you out and trying to lure you to join their organizations. You could be viewed as a rainmaker. You could be viewed as the most eligible bachelor or bachelorette that everyone wants to date or marry; it is much better than being one of hundreds of applicants pursuing a single job.

Your sphere of influence may tout your availability as a once in a lifetime or once every ten year opportunity to hire you! This will be specially true if you have a history of lengthy tenures with organizations. They may even promote your availability in such terms! They may write to others to nominate you for opportunities; such nominations with personal endorsements are far more powerful than blind job applications.

You will find that when you arrive for job interviews with credible endorsements and a publicly verifiable body of work, accolades, and accomplishments, your interviewers will be far more interested in making their organization appealing to you instead of the other way around!

In a typical job interview situation, the organization and the interviewers wield a lot of power. Typical interviewees arrive at a job interview with a significant disadvantage. However, your personal brand can offset this power disadvantage. Even if you do not arrive with the upper hand, you will at least arrive with equal power and your entire interview experience will be collegial and bilateral.

Organizations know they will face significant competition for your services and will make faster and more generous offers. You will also have a stronger negotiating advantage after a job offer. Even if they cannot match your request immediately, they will be willing to make future raise commitments in writing. I observed and experienced all these phenomena firsthand; and the learning has been indelibly seared into my brain.

3.9 INDEPENDENT SOURCE OF POWER

In the traditional world, our jobs, the organizations we work for, and the positions we hold, determine our level of power, income, and value. Sometimes they even determine our status in society. When that job is lost or we separate from the organization, our value sinks dramatically; we may be thrown off balance psychologically.

In the traditional world, most people rely on traditional networks such as alumni associations, fraternities, and sororities. These associations are helpful in job searches and for uncovering opportunities that are never advertised. The hidden job market contains more than half of all job opportunities. In the new digital world, our ability to create a powerful global network is infinite and global in nature. Such digital presence will catch the eye of many recruiters and hiring managers and you will get job offers you never even applied for!

Our opportunities can be global and far beyond the limited boundaries of the organizations we may serve. We must develop these networks using our own personally branded email addresses and phone numbers because we have better control over these. You should not give out business cards or contact information to professional connections containing solely organizational email addresses and phone numbers; it might be okay to share them in addition to contact information you control.

Every connection is valuable. We must always appreciate that connections happen between people. We should always attempt to create a permanent connection with anyone we meet. This is also why connecting on a business social media forum immediately is vital. If we give out business cards with only organizational email addresses and phone numbers, what happens when we lose control or access to these systems?

What if someone else starts to respond on your behalf? Of course, many contacts will be for the new person in your role. However, a large proportion of messages are likely to be specifically for you. Certainly, if the organization is professional enough to provide an auto response with your new contact information, you will have some protection. However, most organizations will not do this.

In fact, organizations will try their hardest to suppress the fact that you are no longer there. This will be specially true if they were benefiting financially from your association with the organization! They may continue promoting your accomplishments and contributions to continue selling their services! They may view your departure as a reputation loss for them! They may even claim you as an alumnus employee to restore some of the lost shine.

Organizations have begun to recognize the brand value of employees. Hence, they will often attempt to suppress an employee's personal brand development. They may prevent you from working part-time with other organizations. Be incredibly careful about agreeing to anything limiting your income streams. Organizations do not own you for all hours of your day and night. Unless you have a guaranteed contract with fair termination clauses like professional athletes, and receive sufficient compensation for exclusivity, should you give your employers the right to deny you the ability to reduce your risks of a layoff?

Sometimes, organizations will discourage an employee from going to a conference to speak. Sometimes organizations will suppress this by providing no budget for professional activities. Sometimes, they will place restrictions on the contents of a business card. The Marketing department of one organization would not allow Dr. to be placed in front of my name citing editorial preference. I told them, I decide how my name is displayed - not them; I printed my own cards at my own expense. We always have a choice which business card we give out to professional contacts we meet!

Taking vacation time to represent ourselves may well pay off in the long run. I had to do this several times. If we are taking personal time to attend a professional event, we should also consider suppressing the organizational name in our speaker profile as well as in our presentation slides and conference interactions. Is there any reason to give an organization the benefit of free advertisement and promotion if the organization is not paying for it in any way and is trying to suppress your professional growth?

In general, I do not allow organizations to limit my ability to grow my personal brand or maintain my independent sources of power! When I negotiated my attendance, I simply asked my organizations whether my attendance would be considered as work time or my personal time and if they wanted the free advertisement or not. In almost all cases, the host conferences that invited me were covering all the expenses anyway.

I rarely spoke at events without bringing in revenue to my employing organization! Even getting the name of the organization on the conference website and agenda is free organizational brand promotion and has earned media value! The power of an organization's name being called out in front of several thousand people during speaker introductions or awards, is earned media gold! In many cases, I was the first person from some programs or organizations to ever keynote a particular conference or receive an award in front of several thousand attendees!

The earned media benefits of these activities are priceless! At many conferences I was the only speaker from my organization. Without my participation as a speaker, the organization's name and the associated revenue benefits would never materialize; these appearances occurred without the massive expenses of paying for a conference booth, which are often as high as $80,000 or higher!

A credible invited speaking slot is a far better draw at a conference than a vendor booth! Vendor booths staffed with marketing personnel may help gain overall brand name recognition for an organization. However, the typical return on investment is dismal.

This is specially true for universities. Prospective students and parents want to hear from faculty and program leaders - not marketing people who cannot answer pedagogical questions. Pairing faculty with marketing does work better. I have often converted a chance meeting into an enrollment within 15 minutes because I matched a prospective student's past background and future goals to the correct academic program. A marketing person can never do this!

My method of framing the question to my employers is powerful and liberating. I would never want my employers to decide whether I can accept a speaking invitation or a professional development opportunity. My employers are not in charge of my professional growth and learning activities. I am. My employers are not responsible for maintaining my certifications, or my continuous learning. I am.

While many employers do support employee professional development, unfortunately the trend over the last forty years has not been healthy. Even at educational institutions where current knowledge is essential, university administrators have been reducing and even eliminating this investment in their faculty. Therefore, everyone must be vigilant to protect themselves against professional atrophy.

Since most employment today can be terminated at will and for no cause, everyone must ensure they remain current and relevant in their chosen fields. This is the only way to protect ourselves from layoff risks. My employers are not responsible for maintaining or growing the value of my personal brand. I am! Therefore, reframing my question to my employer results in fewer instances where I am forced to use my personal time for professional work that would benefit the employer organization far more than it would benefit me.

Such reframing removes my supervisor or employer's financial power and their decision power related to my participation. I should not need permission from anyone to decide whether I would accept or reject a speaking invitation; in many cases the time window for accepting a major opportunity is short. Since I prenegotiated and clarified my thought leadership activities transparently with employers before accepting employment, changes to the agreement after employment can never be acceptable – even if there is a supervisory change! Our personal brand independence must always be guarded zealously!

Since speakers with strong personal brands sell attendance tickets, most respectable organizations and hosts treat speakers like celebrities and cover expenses and even provide respectable honorariums. Cultivating these independent sources of income also insures against career risks. We must always remember that people with strong personal brands are asked to speak at events because of their personal brands and not because of their role in any organization. So, employer organizations stand to gain far more financially than we gain personally.

Once we establish a strong personal brand, our personal brand will become a powerful source of independent power, which can be used to offset, counterbalance, and neutralize organizational sources of power higher than our own. Once established, separation from any organization will affect the organization financially far more than it will ever affect us. Our personal brand may have added credibility and glitz to an organization or a program. Therefore, separation will hurt the organizational finances immediately. We must never forget that we always bring in far more revenue annually than we ever receive in compensation!

Our value independence from employer organizations will also result in rapid discovery of alternative employment opportunities. For us, this phenomenon by itself can mean a higher level of job security and better treatment by organizations and their executives. The more salient and obvious this phenomenon, the higher will be our job security.

A powerful benefit of independence from an organizational brand means that our opportunities will continue even if we are separated from an organization for whatever reason. I was amazed to learn that most people do not keep track of when I join or depart from an organization -- even months or years after my departure!

This phenomenon had a prolonged effect because organizations made no obvious efforts to remove my information from their websites or actively tell people about my departure. Marketing folks know people with name recognition drive traffic to their organizational websites! In general, organizations are therefore very reluctant to remove the names of people with strong personal brands from their websites.

CHAPTER 4

Why Do We Need a Personal Brand?

In the previous section, we understood what a personal brand is. We also learned an important question every employer asks: Is the value of this person higher than what I will pay for the person? Most importantly, we understood that someone's perceived brand value affects how much an organization will be willing to pay that person.

Since most of these concepts have been explained in detail earlier, this section summarizes key tangible benefits of developing a strong personal brand.

4.1 BUILD INCREASED VALUE FOR YOUR WORK

The value of anything is determined by the perception of others. The same item is valued differently by different people. The stronger your personal brand the higher people will perceive the value of your work to be. Even a simple signature can increase the value of something in direct proportion to the value of that person's personal brand.

4.2 HELP MARKET YOUR IDEAS

Your credibility is also directly proportional to your personal brand. Strangely enough, a person with a strong personal brand can increase the market attractiveness of almost any product even if the product is not related to their profession or area of expertise. Therefore, TV and movie personalities are frequently used to market various products. Even actors who never finished college have been used successfully to market colleges simply because of their personal brand and name recognition.

4.3 DEVELOP CONFIDENCE AND JOB SECURITY

Most often other people control whether you can stay in a job. However, a strong personal brand will give you better job security and in the event of a job separation it will help you to find another job faster. When you are in control, you can carry yourself with greater confidence and can manage your career risks better.

4.4 GAIN BETTER CONTROL OF YOUR CAREER

A strong personal brand may deter employers from mistreating you. They may be more fearful of the financial consequences of laying you off and may be more willing to continuously increase your compensation due to the increasing value you bring to the organization. When you ask for raises, you will have stronger tangible financial arguments to support your requests for such raises.

4.5 CREATE MULTIPLE SOURCES OF INCOME

A strong personal brand will create multiple revenue streams for you, such as book royalties, speaking fees, endorsements, sponsorships, paid advisory board roles, consulting fees, fees for reviewing materials, and income from personal coaching and mentoring. The possibilities are endless! Such diversification of income streams reduces your career risks - like diversification in your investment portfolio.

4.6 INCREASE EARNINGS

Of course, as your opportunities and income sources increase, your overall earnings will also increase. You will continue to grow in multiple intellectual dimensions because your brain will be perpetually challenged in a wide range of dimensions. You will find yourself becoming conversant in an ever expanding range of issues surrounding your passion. This phenomenon will increase the value of your personal brand even further; this virtuous cycle will increasingly benefit you financially!

4.7 DECOUPLE PERSONAL SUCCESS FROM ORGANIZATIONS

Once personal success is decoupled from organizations, a single organization will no longer have a significant grip on your income, life, and wellbeing. Organizations will have a higher incentive to pay you according to the value you produce. Thus, your personal brand will become an important source of power far beyond the limits of organizational sources of power. Since your personal success is not dependent on an organization, you will be in a stronger position to walk away from exploitative, unfair, or unethical situations.

WHY BUILD A PERSONAL BRAND?

Build Increased Value for Your Work
Help Market Your Ideas
Develop Confidence and Job Security
Gain Better Control of Your Career
Create Multiple Sources of Income
Increase Earnings
Personal Success Decoupled from Organization

Why Build a Personal Brand?

CHAPTER 5

How Do We Build a Personal Brand?

Now that you understand the need to build a personal brand and what it can do for you, let us focus on how you can build your personal brand using the following seven steps.

PERSONAL BRAND IN SEVEN STEPS

Discover You
Embrace You
Bring Inner Greatness Out
Embrace Discomfort as the First Step to Greatness
Embrace Greatness as a Practiced Art
Become Charismatic
Protect the Value of Your Personal Brand

Personal Brand in Seven Steps

5.1 DISCOVER YOU

Greatness is a choice. Greatness already exists in everyone. You just need to let it out. Societal expectations to conform will suppress this

48

greatness. Society will make you afraid to let it out. You will be socially programmed to avoid being the first to do anything. You will often be held back with, "What will people think?"

Yet, greatness can only be achieved by taking risks, by being the first to do anything, by embracing your vulnerabilities, and by revealing as much of yourself as you dare! If you worry too much about what people think, you will suppress your greatness.

Greatness is a journey. Self-discovery and expression to the world need to be incremental. With each step you will become more comfortable. The journey begins with the discovery of your unique gifts and talents, figuring out what you enjoy, and then focusing methodically on bringing that inner greatness out.

The process will seem risky and uncomfortable. However, as you continue to do more of it, you will become comfortable with it. Being the first to do anything is the start of the journey to greatness. Always remember that if some risky innovation does not work out, you have the power never to do it again. *Knowing what does not work is just as important as knowing what works.*

In the previous section, you understood some key elements of a personal brand. You also went through a self-discovery process by listing your values, your mission, the causes you support, and all the elements that will make up your personal brand. *Now put some key elements together and develop an elevator pitch, which you should be able to use to introduce yourself to anyone within one to two minutes.*

Do you like the way your pitch sounds? If not, keep working on it until you do. Try it a few times with new people you meet. Does your introduction cause people to be interested in you and ask you questions? Do they want to learn more about you? Does it start to build some instant connection? Do they even find you compelling or inspiring?

Create one to two minute videos and pass them around to your trusted network. Do they like it? Do they have suggestions? What reactions do you get from strangers?

5.1.1 Turn Off the Excuses

You are shy until you aren't. You are an introvert until you aren't. While these words exist, too much reliance on them as excuses can be major psychological obstacles to your greatness. Therefore, understanding the psychology of shyness or introversion is extremely important.

In modern society, our fear of failure or our fear of doing or saying something wrong or embarrassing are the key reasons why we hold ourselves back. Our brains and chemical reactions are programmed to view these as social threats. We brand ourselves as shy or introverted to rationalize our decisions.

However, both words simply describe choices. We should not let these words define us. We need these impulses to help us make rational decisions on the way we dress or behave according to the situation. The key is to understand that we can recalibrate our choices to better reflect rational thinking.

Risks usually have rewards. Our propensity to take a risk is increased by mitigating the dangers. We can apply risk mitigation techniques to reduce the risks such that the benefits far outweigh the risks. For example, driving a car is a dangerous activity. However, we take lessons, take tests, obtain licenses, put on seat belts, install airbags, drive within lanes, maintain speed, stay alert, and implement many other risk mitigation choices so we can enjoy the benefits of driving.

As we practice and improve our skills at anything, our shyness and fear of failure at that activity will subside. While our knees may shake and our voices may tremble the first time we stand in front of an audience, these reactions will disappear once we figure out that we do survive these situations and there is no reason to fear them. Our brains will be reprogrammed to view these situations as welcome opportunities and not threats!

We all have natural chemical defense mechanisms designed to save us from life threatening situations. These chemicals protected us during the cave human days by ensuring that we would hide from danger. Staying silent was always less risky. Avoiding confrontation usually worked in our favor. The same chemical defenses are activated by social threats.

In our modern civilized society these chemical defenses are usually not required anymore; social threats are not usually life threatening. In addition, we have lots of risk mitigation techniques. However, these reactions do exist in all of us. The good news is that we can learn to control these impulses; we can make rational decisions about our choices without relying on pure primordial impulses.

However, we must understand the two following principles:

1) People who do nothing will never make a mistake.
2) People who say nothing will never say anything wrong.

Therefore, anyone who acts and speaks will make errors. Statistically if people fail 10% of the time, a person who does one hundred things will fail at ten things. However, the person who does only ten things will fail at only one! Instead of focusing on the ten failures, why shouldn't we focus on the ninety successes? The key is to reduce the percentage of errors and to develop ways to recover from errors through training and practice.

You will often hear someone say, "I used to be shy," or "I am really an introvert." They might say this immediately after delivering an excellent presentation in front of hundreds of people. Essentially, what they are saying is that they have successfully recalibrated their brains and chemical responses to make more rational calculations of social threats.

We all have degrees of shyness and introversion and such impulses protect us from completely inappropriate behavior choices. However, let's not rely on these types of crutch words to hold back our greatness. Greatness is a choice and all other choices we make, must work in harmony to support our choice to Bring Inner Greatness Out!

5.2 EMBRACE YOU

Too many people do not like themselves enough. They do not even want to appear in photographs or videos; they keep the camera turned off even during a video meeting. They do not believe in themselves.

Sometimes, they try to be someone else; they try to emulate someone else. They look at others and feel inadequate or are frozen in awe. Sometimes they compare themselves with someone with decades of experience and knowledge in a field they are starting out.

However, by focusing on others they lose focus in themselves. While it is okay to be inspired by others and to incorporate ideas from other people into your own persona, in general it is far easier to be yourself. Comparing yourself with someone with far more experience and education than yourself is unfair to you. Focus on yourself - not on others!

You already start with powerful uniqueness. There is only one you in the entire world. Think about that for a moment. In this world of several billion people, there is no one else like you. So, the supply is already low. Doesn't simple economics tell us that the price of something with low supply should be high? Therefore, theoretically your brand value is infinite - all depends on the level of demand you can create.

Your inherent uniqueness gives you a powerful starting point. Why not monetize the true value of this uniqueness. *You do not need to be perfect; you need to perfect your uniqueness.* Your uniqueness includes all natural perceived imperfections you inherited when you were born. Your imperfections can even be the initial distinguishing characteristics of your personal brand!

Your so called imperfection or deficiency could become your greatest strength. The key is to embrace yourself and then continuously impart incremental value to yourself by developing your skills through training, education, experiences, and innovation. Think of it as packaging yourself. The better the packaging, the higher your perceived value.

Packaging includes how you walk, feel, and talk about yourself. It also includes your personal grooming, vocal variety, diction, demeanor, and most importantly the substance of what you say and write. You have total control over all these things. As you improve your packaging, you will see your value rise - just like magic!

The way you package yourself will also have a psychological impact on you. You will feel better, act better, execute better, and have a much higher level of confidence in yourself. Such confidence is critical. If you think you can, you will. Lack of confidence will be debilitating.

I mention perceived imperfections because all our so called imperfections are based on societal expectations of what is normal. For example, in a society where being born a man may be perceived as a strength, being born a woman may be perceived as a weakness. Similarly, being visually or physically different may be perceived as a disadvantage. We need to abandon this type of thinking! *We need to accept what we cannot change and focus on things we can change!*

Greatness is achieved when we embrace our perceived weaknesses or imperfections and project these as our greatest strengths. For example, only someone whose vision is impaired can experience the world of the blind. If this world needs to be described to other blind people, who better than a blind person to do this?

I once explained this concept to one of my visually impaired students. After learning how he had solved his learning hurdles, I urged him to write and share his experiences and lead the way for others who have similar challenges. I mentioned how, if he chose to act on my suggestions, his journey of leading others with similar perceived weaknesses could rebrand him and his perceived weakness into his greatest strength.

I told him instead of viewing his situation as a disability - the terminology used by people who have a different view of what normal is - he should view it as his greatest strength because only he has the unique ability to share the experiences of his world. By taking this journey, he would unleash his own greatness! After our conversation, he told me his perception and outlook changed forever! You too must think this way!

5.2.1 *Turning Disadvantages to Greatest Strengths*

Society often calls some people disabled or disadvantaged. However, people who have accepted what they cannot control and have focused on what they can control, to surpass personal and societal expectations, are neither disabled nor disadvantaged. In fact, by surpassing expectations, they have just demonstrated how great they really are. *Instead of focusing on what we cannot do, we must focus on what we can do!*

Every adversity is an opportunity to bring out greatness. In solving every problem, we rise to the next level. My father abandoned us when I was in the seventh grade. This event created a serious financial crisis in our family lives; for the longest time, I lamented this event. However, this event also forced me to seek ways to make money at a far earlier age than all my classmates and friends.

In seventh grade, I used art, language, and poetry skills to make hand painted greeting cards with messages in rhymes. Commercial cards were non-existent. My adversity turned into a unique opportunity for me to start my first small business. In the tenth grade, once I was old enough to travel alone, I began tutoring younger students in their homes.

These initiatives created significant multiple streams of income, which were unusual for someone my age. Soon, what should have been a weakness became my greatest strength. Many years later as I reflected on my life events, instead of being angry at my father, I was able to forgive and celebrate his early exit from my life. *The key is to ensure that adversity does not define us; instead, let the solution define us!*

5.2.1.1 Pivot Points

We should treat all adversities as pivot points and forks in our journey through life. Most adversities are completely out of our control and happen due to the actions of others. Some are acts of nature. We can choose to lament our situation, or we can choose to solve the problem using skills and tools over which we have total control.

People often focus on problems and get bogged down in self-blame for the problems -- even though these problems are the direct result of other people's actions -- over which they have zero control. This misplaced backward focus can be debilitating and can prevent someone from finding solutions. *Do not focus on problems; focus on solutions!*

When people focus on the problem, they lose sight of the solution! Rather than worry too much about why a problem happened, I always focus on the solution -- primarily looking for solutions which depend solely upon my own actions -- over which I have 100% control.

Sometimes, the answers are not the most obvious ones. Sometimes, the choices involve heading towards a risky path -- since it involves innovation. While these choices may involve risks, innovation always has major opportunities for gain. Certainly, they are likely to lead to interesting adventures.

Pivot points are normal; they force us to choose a different path. On the surface, pivot points may appear to be problems. If we focus on the problems, we can be destroyed. Instead, if we focus on the solutions, and open our minds to all possibilities, we can take our lives and careers towards a far more exciting and meaningful direction. To explain this, let me share two major pivot points of my career.

During the early 1980s, I was a PhD student of Political Science at Emory University in Atlanta, Georgia. Here, I learned to analyze large amounts of research data using computers. I also learned to build local area networks. I was close to graduation and ready to settle into my predictable life as a professor of Political Science.

Suddenly, I learned, my dissertation chair was denied tenure and was moving to another university in another state. My new dissertation chair asked me to change my dissertation; my topic was not in her area of expertise or interest. Therefore, I faced two choices: Change my dissertation, or change the direction of my life.

I reasoned that the world already had plenty of PhDs in Political Science but hardly any network engineers or digital strategists. So, I decided to change the direction of my life. I moved to Texas to modernize a medical college with a teaching hospital from paper records to electronic records, electronic research, word processing, electronic spreadsheets, digital printing, and of course email.

As I walked around, met people, and discussed ideas, I saw many concerned faces. These people had been earning a living as typists, key punch operators; some performed accounting and payroll tasks using calculators, and thick paper ledgers. They had seen previous technology adoption lead to waves of layoffs.

Layoffs never made sense to me! So, I made a bold promise - there would be no layoffs. Everyone would be trained and transitioned into the new environment. Their careers would take an exciting and more financially rewarding turn because they will be the first in the state of Texas to be experts in the new technology. I personally trained four hundred of the five hundred employees and unleashed a culture of innovation and productivity. I learned an important lesson – the true power of technology is not in replacing people, but in how much more productive and innovative it makes people.

I moved to Maryland to join a massive project to modernize the Calvert Cliffs Nuclear Power Plant, which had 2,500 people. The Plant had been put on a watch list because they had rooms full of paper records and no way to retrieve anything quickly. My job was to build the enterprise network and the governance and support environment. A model for this did not exist anywhere in the world!

Guided by my values and who I am, once again, I embraced people. Our investments in the network and the technology could never be successful if people did not know how to use the network effectively to be more productive and innovative in their jobs! My team and I - just three of us - trained a hundred people from one hundred organizational units across the Plant as super users. In turn, they trained and supported all the people in their units. The productivity and innovation we unleashed were unimaginable! We also earned an extraordinary amount of goodwill!

A few years later, I arrived at another major pivot point. I was Chief Information Officer at a state biotechnology research university. I had been there for almost a decade and the job seemed secure. Then in 2009 our President was abruptly laid off. The university was shut down because it was losing money during an economic downturn and various parts of the university were carved up and given to other universities.

In January of 2010, I was laid off along with the rest of the entire executive team. To cope, I relied on the same simple principle I had learned early in life, which I have shared with you in this book: While we have zero control over the actions of others, we have 100% control over our own actions and reactions. *Do not focus on the problem; focus on possible solutions that rely solely upon your own actions.*

I took a step back to sort out my options carefully. While looking for jobs, I spoke at conferences and attended every free conference I learned about. I also visited universities and travelled throughout the United States. After all, never, did I ever have such an extraordinary supply of time in my hands. I looked at the university curriculum and absorbed what was going on in the worlds of technology, business, and education.

At one of these conferences, I learned of a new online Doctor of Science program in Information Assurance (the old name for Cybersecurity) catering to full-time working professionals. I also learned that I was perfectly qualified to join this program. I joined the program and, for my doctoral dissertation, conducted a national study of cybersecurity in US healthcare and published my first book Impact of Security Culture in Security Compliance in Healthcare in the USA.

During this time, I learned about the world of commercial publishing, which is skewed in favor of publishers. I also learned about the world of independent publishing, which is skewed in favor of authors and readers. I chose independent publishing to ensure everyone could buy my books without worrying about spending a lot of money. This choice also gave me the freedom to publish ebook, paperback, and audio versions of my book and distribute the works globally without any restrictions.

In 2013, I graduated as one of the first few in the world with a doctoral degree in cybersecurity. This journey also made me realize how broken everything is from university education, business hiring, business leadership, to even the teaching of cybersecurity in university degree programs.

Students were graduating knowing things, but they could not do things in the real world! Organizations did not want to train them. Executives and TV pundits were using terms such as "skills gap" to explain away critical vacant positions. People with college degrees in cybersecurity were being overlooked because hiring managers either had prior bad experiences with fresh college graduates or had no clue who to hire or how to train and mentor them. The hiring gap continued to grow wider. Yet, it appeared too many people did not understand the cybersecurity field.

So, I published the book Cybersecurity Leadership: Powering the Modern Organization to help everyone from high school students to corporate executives to understand the field and to learn how to build successful and profitable modern organizations through a people powered perpetual innovation culture, empowered by technology. In October 2015 at CyberMaryland, I announced Master and Doctor of Science programs in cybersecurity with a blend of business, analytics, leadership, and communications to help universities fix their academic programs.

I became passionate about sharing knowledge and helping others succeed. To me this was the essence of leadership! I have always felt leaders should not only point out problems but also offer solutions. I published hundreds of articles, interviews, media commentaries, and accepted almost every invitation to speak so I could share knowledge and empower others.

I always believed in the key principle of capitalism that if you work hard and you innovate, you will enjoy the fruits of your hard work and innovation. I have also believed that compensation should be proportional to contribution and not according to organizational power and rank.

However, I observed that unethical people in positions of power were usurping most of the profits of companies for themselves, while leaving the actual producers of profit in a perpetual state of uncertainty and subsistence. Working hard was not leading to a better life. Even basic home ownership and education were becoming unaffordable to a large segment of the population.

Capitalism was turning into an oligarchy. Monopolies were killing competition. Large corporate giants were destroying free labor markets with non-compete agreements and secret labor market fixing arrangements so they could dictate below market compensation for all workers.

They were also holding workers hostage with employment connected healthcare; a layoff also means loss of healthcare.

Even though companies appeared profitable on the surface, employee disengagement, churn, lack of allegiance, and a culture of perpetual layoffs were suppressing an even larger amount of profits for these companies. Executives were oblivious to this phenomenon because they themselves were doing very well. Yet, readily available research data showed that innovation in the US had become half of what it used to be in the 1970s.

I always saw cybersecurity as people powered perpetual innovation and the key to organizational success. I also knew that without ethical leadership we can never get there. Ethical leadership is the principle of sharing the fruits of success with the people who produced that success! If organizational executives do not practice ethical leadership, we can never achieve a culture of people powered perpetual innovation. Ethical leadership is the foundation of capitalism!

During these two major pivot points of my life, I remained true to who I am, preserved my values, focused on what I could control while accepting what I could not control and turned adversities into opportunities. I was open to risks as well as redirecting the very trajectory of my life and career; suddenly, the disadvantages transformed into my greatest strengths.

Therefore, embrace yourself. Love who you are and take care of yourself. If you do not accept and love yourself, why would anyone else? Celebrate the uniqueness and the circumstances of your birth, upbringing, and everything else that you could never control.

You may have been abandoned at birth. You may have been adopted and may never have met your birth parents. You may have been bullied, body shamed, or worse. However, you could not control these situations. Reach harder for your inner greatness. If you have already survived, why not celebrate that you overcame the challenges; you worked hard to achieve who you are today? Without your adversity you would never have been who you are today!

If you have not overcome the challenges yet, dig deeper into the possibilities. You will find solutions. You will be stronger as you solve the problems. There are people in far worse situations.

Your life could have been far worse if the adversities did not happen in your life. You would have been a different person altogether! By embracing, accepting, forgiving, and moving past the negative situations of your life, you will be able to gain control over the adversity instead of allowing it to control you! Focus on the solution, not the problem.

You cannot control the actions of others or various events that happen around you. However, you do have 100% control over your own actions and reactions. So, take charge and step forward! Your greatness awaits! There is no one in the world like you. Embrace that! Celebrate that! Make that the starting point of your journey to greatness!

5.2.1.2 Student Success Stories Applying This Principle

I joined UMUC as Chair of the Master of Science in Cybersecurity Technology Program in April of 2016. During my 3.5 year stint, I had a front row seat watching thousands of students transform from possibilities into realities. I have shared a few noteworthy stories below.

5.2.1.2.1 A Thanksgiving Dinner

While teaching my very first cohort of students, I was very intrigued by a project report submitted by a student named Naalphatu Toure. The substance was excellent, but the writing needed work to be acceptable at the graduate level. My principle in teaching has always been to cater to the individual needs of every student in my class.

I also do not believe in giving students a single attempt at a project. In the real workplace, we usually get to review drafts with others to receive constructive feedback. The goal should be to evaluate a student on their final level of competency and not their starting point.

Simply failing a student or just assigning a grade helps no one and is a disservice to the student. I feel professors are just as responsible for student success as the students. Professors should not be judges; they need to be coaches and mentors. Therefore, I always make extra effort to learn about each student to coach and mentor them according to their specific situation.

This is even more important in an adult learner environment where people from all ages and walks of life are in the same class. At open universities with relaxed admission requirements we must work harder to cater to each student. So, I asked Naalphatu to call me at her leisure.

During the call I explained that her analysis and technical content were strong. However, her primary problem was writing, and we needed to work on this. By choosing to use the pronoun "we" I did not dump the problem on her alone!

While I could help to a certain extent, I told her she needed to work on this with some extra tutoring or coaching. So, I asked if she was aware of the free Writing Center services available from the university and if she had ever used it.

I was shocked by what I learned during this conversation:

1. She was repeating the class because her previous instructor for this class had failed her for .5 points.
2. She had never talked with her professor during the entire term.
3. The professor never mentioned her weakness in the English language or told her about the Writing Center.
4. The professor never let her know that she was missing some assignments, which would have immediately increased her score.
5. When she contacted the professor after learning her final grade, he simply said, "You are not prepared for the course or program. Naalphatu, as far as I am concerned this is a closed issue."

What happened here is typical of many universities, students, and professors - specially in an online format. Too many online professors never talk with a student. Too many professors do not care about the person or the dreams behind every student.

Our job isn't simply to judge and score a student's work. We must provide actionable feedback and provide every student with the required teaching, mentoring, and coaching to help them succeed! I went to work with Naalphatu and told her the following:

1. Celebrate the previous incident. Do not be ashamed of it because it was a failure of the professor; in my opinion the professor did not do his job. Being in my class might turn out to be an important pivot point in her life. Sometimes we focus on a bad incident and never realize that the bad incident brought us to an even better possibility. If she had not failed in the previous class, she would not have joined my class and our paths might never have crossed!

2. Never turn away or hide from the negative things that may have happened. Instead, talk about how she solved the problems to overcome the negative things. That will give her power over those things. I also shared bits of my stories.

3. She had greatness inside her; without that greatness she could not have accomplished what she had already accomplished. Bumps on the road are normal and we must always look at the additional possibilities each bump creates. We must keep the tools handy to fix the flat tires of our lives.

4. To me she was like an unpolished diamond. It was my job to turn her talent into a polished diamond so she can sparkle. Do everything I suggest. Do all the work in the class - and I will keep track if she is missing anything. She can rest assured that students who do the work I require in my classes have never failed. It may require a little extra effort and more than one attempt, but she must do all the work. However, she should not be afraid to try. Such fears are unnecessary in my classes.

5. Submit everything to the Writing Center before submitting to me. Work with them on the writing for anything she writes for her entire time as a student - not just my class. This will help

her build the strong foundation she will need to be tremendously successful as a professional in the field.

6. Attend every free conference I suggest, learn, and network outside the classroom. This habit will help her learn perpetually.

7. While I will work with the professor separately and monitor that he does not damage other students by shirking his duties, she can rest assured that no future professor will be able to treat her in the same manner as long as I remain Chair. I will always be a phone call or an email away and she will receive a response from me within hours - maximum 24 hours!

8. I would be a mentor for her for as long as she needed - even after my class.

Naalphatu Toure did everything I suggested, graduated from the program with distinction in 2018 along with Tomiko Evans, and was invited to join the Upsilon Pi Epsilon honor society because of her academic record. She was on fire!

Tomiko Evans, Maureen Bunyan, Naalphatu Toure, 2018

She networked at conferences and was invited to share her story at several events. She completed an MBA degree immediately after graduating from my program. In February of 2020, she placed first in a Capture the Flag contest at a cybersecurity conference and became a mentor to a university's ethical hacking club! Today she has a brand of her own as the #InternationalCybersecurityAficionado and has launched the website https://cypeeps.com/ with her friend Thelma Muronzi.

She shared her own story in a blog because she understood the key principle in life I teach everyone: While We Cannot Change the Past We Can Change the Future. In writing this blog and in sharing this story at conferences, she took control of this negative incident instead of letting the incident control her.

She embraced her greatness with confidence and showed everyone that her bad professor was wrong about her! Other people's opinions did not define her limitations. She was made for greatness - all she needed was the right teacher and mentor. She was not only prepared for the course and the program, but ready to be a great leader in the field of cybersecurity!

As a member of the Cybersecurity Divas 2020 Global Tour, in front of a global audience, she displayed her innovation and leadership with an amazing presentation showing how gamification could be used to make cybersecurity education fun. This was her second major conference presentation in addition to several others. I have remained a mentor for her to this day and I continue to enjoy watching her Bring Inner Greatness Out! She also joined us for a Thanksgiving dinner with other international students.

5.2.1.2.2 Exercising the Brain

Katoria Henry called me one day to explain her frustration with the workload in the program. Like many students, she was shell shocked with the amount of work. She was working full-time, and this is not what she experienced at other online programs; online programs should be easier.

I calmly explained to Katoria that the entire program is interconnected. Every course builds upon the other, which is why we only accept transfer credit for one course. I had purposely designed the program so that they could graduate with confidence that they went through a solid program. Reducing the workload will weaken her mental development and slow down her success after graduation.

I explained that her brain was just like a muscle; initially the class feels harder because the brain is being stretched and will develop many new neurological connections that will serve her well for the rest of her life. "Yes, the workload is heavy. But every project is there to develop a different aspect of your brain. You will need these competencies to be successful as a cybersecurity professional," I explained. I shared my own background as a practitioner for more than thirty years and my knowledge of the job market.

"Do not complain about the workload. If it is too easy, your brain will not develop further. At this point you may not appreciate what the entire program will give you. So, you will need to trust that we did the right thing to prepare you well. Put your head down for now and trust that I have sincerely developed the best cybersecurity program in the world.

Nothing like this program exists anywhere in the world. Focus on graduation as you will be among the first to graduate from this program. I will personally be your mentor; your success is also my success. Once you graduate, you will be able to write your own ticket to success. We cannot reduce the work without watering down the program. Things will get easier after the first course because your brain will get over the initial shock. By the time you graduate, you will see that your brain is operating at a different level," I said.

Luckily, Katoria trusted me and never complained again. We had many conversations on the phone and email. Then on the day of Katoria Henry's graduation, I made it a point to find her in the graduation line. I finally met her in person for the first time ever - in her graduation robe. We took a picture together to commemorate our mutual achievement. Then I asked her, "How do you feel about your brain now Katoria?"

Katoria Henry Graduation, 2018

Without flinching a second, she replied with a hearty laugh, "Oh, Dr. Hasib, I can whip out one of those papers in fifteen minutes now!" That remains one of my most memorable moments as a teacher! I could sense her greatness had been unleashed and she was confident in her greatness; this confidence will serve her well. I had done my job! It was truly a moment of mutual success.

Not only did Katoria Henry find her greatness, she went on to write the ticket to her career as I had suggested. While still a graduate student, she took on additional responsibilities at her place of work at a major federal agency and created a position for herself that allowed her to use her learning in school; she also obtained raises through sheer hard work and leadership.

In the cybersecurity community she established a brand for herself as #NISTBarbie. She is a nominee and finalist for some awards and currently serves as the Security Governance Risk and Compliance Manager for Salesforce. She also made two excellent presentations with the Cybersecurity Divas. In one of these presentations, she used a sportscaster theme and humor to make an excellent innovative presentation.

She continues to be a sought after speaker, leader, and role model for others in the field.

5.2.1.2.3 Real Estate to Cybersecurity Auditing

One evening, I was attending the networking hour at a practitioner oriented conference. Most professors and academic leaders never attend these events; they usually attend pure academic conferences working to build their curriculum vitae for tenure. However, this is not where the prospective students are.

The largest group of prospective students is at business and professional practice oriented conferences. Many are not actively exploring more education. Until they meet the right person and understand what a program can do for them, they will never enroll. Many are not aware that they can pursue education while continuing to work full-time.

As a social butterfly, I work the room at any conference. I sauntered over to a US Navy Captain, dressed in full uniform. We chatted about the field of cybersecurity, and I shared my background working in education, healthcare, biotechnology, and energy. I told him I had built an innovative graduate cybersecurity program where we would accept students from any discipline. I also mentioned my goal was to make the program earn the reputation of being the best in the world!

The Captain's son had graduated from The Citadel and was working as a real estate agent and did not have a direction for his life or an inspiration for a career. I invited him to visit our campus with his son and offered to explore his son's interests and suggest possibilities in our various cybersecurity or other graduate programs at the university.

One of the keys to greatness is finding a field to be passionate about. It must not feel like work! We must enjoy what we do so much that we can spend hours at it without feeling tired, stressed, or bored. Thus, I always explore someone's interests and strengths and explain various choices instead of pushing anyone in any direction. I look for the glint in their eyes.

When the Captain and his son arrived, I took time to understand the young man's background and interests. Then, I explained all cybersecurity programs in detail and gave them an overview of other graduate programs at the university. I also explained the teaching models and what he would learn. I reassured him that the program was designed for full-time working professionals.

As I explained the cybersecurity field and the cybersecurity model shared in my book **Cybersecurity Leadership**, I could see the glint in their eyes. The Captain's son recognized that his undergraduate business degree was not a weakness, but a strength. He realized how my program design was really an extension of the business field he loved and enjoyed.

I also explained how his marketing skills in real estate would translate into the cybersecurity field. Having been a real estate agent myself for ten years, I translated everything in terms he easily understood. I explained how my own marketing skills honed during ten years of real estate sales had helped me in my business and academic leadership roles!

The Captain's son immediately became motivated to join the program. Neither of them was aware of these programs or the university teaching models; if they had not met me, they would never have considered this journey. Graduate recruiting is an extremely high touch activity!

In this case, two people had to show up to create an opportunity for a random meeting. The Captain did not have to show up at the networking event; he had already attended the conference sessions. It was certainly not part of my job either. However, networking after a conference is one of the best places to meet interesting people. This has always been my favorite part of any conference.

Once the Captain's son enrolled, I took him into my own class even though my class was already full; I wanted to take care of him personally. The son's transformation was amazing! He found his professional passion in the risk management aspects of cybersecurity! Well before graduation, he landed a job performing cybersecurity audits at the Pentagon!

Since graduation, he has worked with several major consulting firms and his income has doubled since our initial conversation!

5.2.1.3 Embrace Greatness as a Choice

If you believe you are great, you can be great. Your attitude towards yourself is everything. This attitude is controlled in your brain; you have 100% control over your attitude. You have 100% control over what you believe. Your greatness is a choice!

If you examine all the stories I have shared so far, you will notice the key ingredient that made everyone succeed is their belief in their ability to succeed - their belief that they could be great. My focus in working with them was to awaken and nurture this belief and give them the confidence to execute. That is the key job of a mentor, coach, or teacher.

Although everyone is born extraordinary, they may appear ordinary until they choose to do extraordinary things. All ordinary people can do extraordinary things. In doing extraordinary things as a practiced art form, seemingly ordinary people become extraordinary. They do this by discovering and accentuating the uniqueness that already exists in them.

Some people have said that you do not even need to do extraordinary things - just do some extra things that others will not do. I call it bringing your entire unique self to any job or activity. *Do not be defined by what others did. Do it in a manner no one else will!*

As you discover and embrace yourself, you will find that you have many unique interests, talents, and gifts that make you who you are. You should make a written list of all the things you can do and enjoy. You should also list the things you cannot do and do not enjoy. *Learn to focus on what you can do, and not on what you cannot do.* You can capitalize and monetize things you can do.

You will discover stories in your past where you solved problems, became resilient, and overcame adversity. Relive and celebrate the stories of overcoming, instead of lamenting the problems you could not control. By taking control of the stories you will gain powerful control over the events over which you had no control.

As you relive and share these stories, you will feel vulnerable. Initially, such revelations of yourself to the outside world will feel discomforting. However, these revelations will also liberate you from the negative experiences of your life. Instead of these events controlling you and holding you back, you will gain control over these events and propel your rise to your true potential for greatness.

When you face any problem, search for new opportunities presented by the problem. Instead of focusing on and internalizing the negative effects of your problems, you will find yourself creating powerful stories of your greatness; you will create stories of overcoming your problems. Instead of lamenting about problems, you will find yourself excited about the solutions and the future possibilities of your life. This is how inner greatness comes out.

5.2.2 Toastmasters

You will need to hone three key skills to project your inner greatness: leadership, listening, and communication skills. All people are born with these skills; however, they must sharpen these skills through coaching, constructive feedback, and practice. Public speaking can be scary. I have heard many new Toastmasters members say they fear public speaking more than death! Through Toastmasters people learn to believe in themselves!

While fear is normal, Toastmasters International is a global non-profit organization with thousands of local clubs serving neighborhoods all over the world where people can sharpen their leadership, communication, and listening skills. The organization's mission is powerfully captured in the slogan: Where Leaders Are Made.

At many clubs such as the Toast of Severna Park, where I was elected President for the 2020-2021 year, the executive leadership team voted to establish free formal mentoring and coaching programs for new members. Such mentoring accelerates the development of new members and helps them achieve rapid confidence and success. Every club has a culture of its own. Therefore, prospective members should explore multiple clubs before joining one that best meets the environment they feel comfortable with.

Toastmasters members choose a learning path based on their interests and complete projects in their chosen path. Other members observe speeches and leadership activities and provide constructive and actionable feedback that members can use to improve. Many clubs record speeches and evaluations so members can use these additional resources to improve further.

Good communicators are efficient in their use of language; they are also eloquent in their message. Great speeches move people; they inspire people. Quotations from great speeches are circulated by people; the inspiration from these quotes can motivate people globally for decades! Such is the power of effective communications.

Toastmasters speakers also imbue speeches with emotion and take audiences through an emotional journey. No one likes to listen to a boring monologue for one hour. Toastmasters members practice one of my key principles: *Significance is not determined by the amount of time on stage but by what you do with the time you get.*

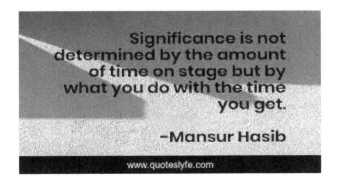

Most Toastmasters speeches are five to seven minutes. Yet, during this short period of time, strong speakers have an opening, body, and a valuable message or a call to action relevant to the audience. Speakers also use gestures, motion, props, compelling language, correct grammar, clear diction, vocal variety, humor, and audience engagement to make their speeches memorable.

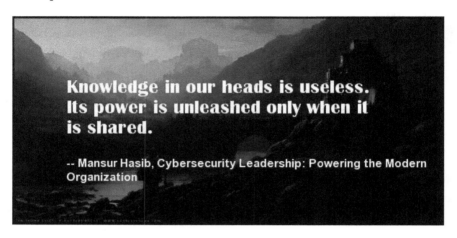

Knowledge in our heads is useless. Its power is unleashed only when it is shared.

-- Mansur Hasib, Cybersecurity Leadership: Powering the Modern Organization

We learn to convey meaning with fewer words, which can have a memorable impact. An amazing free reward of making powerful statements and quotes in public forums, books and writings is that various sites collect and share these quotes - thus amplifying our messages and our personal brands dramatically.

Many of my popular quotes are listed on several sites. To get your quote trending and promoted, create a slide, convert it to an image file, and post it in business social media sites such as Goodreads, LinkedIn, Pinterest, Facebook, or Twitter. If the quotes are original and contain strong memorable messages, they will be picked up by multiple sites. In this hyperconnected era you will be amazed at how quickly this happens.

Everyone can make memorable statements. The key is to be aware of your original quotable quotes. You will develop many of these if you choose to practice in Toastmasters. Sometimes, another member will point out your quotes or messages that resonated with them. Preserve and share these quotes. One day you will be pleasantly surprised to be listed on the same quotation page as Aristotle and Oprah Winfrey!

Significance is not determined by the amount of time on stage but by what you do with the time you get. - *Mansur Hasib*

A note of music gains significance from the silence on either side. - *Anne Morrow Lindbergh*

The aim of art is to represent not the outward appearance of things, but their inward significance. - *Aristotle*

When indeed does the temporal suffering oppress a man most terribly? Is it not when it seems to him that it has no significance, that it neither secures nor gains anything for him? Is it not when the suffering, as the impatient man expresses it, is without meaning or purpose? - *Soren Kierkegaard*

[American] liberalism today sees no realm of human life that is beyond political significance, from what you eat to what you smoke to what you say. - *Jonah Goldberg*

When we abolish the slavery of half of humanity, together with the whole system of hypocrisy it implies, then the "division" of humanity will reveal its genuine significance and the human couple will find its true form. - *Simone de Beauvoir*

The key to realizing a dream is to focus not on success but significance - and then even the small steps and little victories along your path will take on greater meaning. - *Oprah Winfrey*

Quotes for word "significance" on quotes.schollz.com

Toastmasters speeches are evaluated for grammar and effective use of language; speakers must stay within allocated time limits. In addition, speakers are evaluated on their avoidance of speech defects such as "um", "ah", "you know", "like", "so" and other similar noises. Even though many famous orators are guilty of having these defects, eliminating them will dramatically accelerate your success.

Speech defects detract from a speaker's message. When amplified through a microphone, these speech defects sound cacophonous and make the speaker sound amateurish and unprofessional. For audience members, the experience is like suffering through an off key karaoke performance.

Speech defects force the brains of audience members to work extra hard to filter them out to make sense of the message. Thus, audience members will tire or lose interest sooner. Every "um" or similar noise is a jarring interruption in their concentration on your message. These defects will unnecessarily lengthen a speech. Through practice, Toastmasters members expunge such defects from their speeches and give their audiences impactful mellifluous listening experiences.

Good speakers may replace such defects with pauses, gestures, movement, or powerful anticipatory silence. Do not be afraid or uncomfortable with silence. Pauses and moments of silence, help audience members stay zoned in on a speaker's message. Instead of tiring out their brains filtering out speech defects, they eagerly await the speaker's next sentence. They stop playing with their smartphones or texting friends. A speaker's silence is powerful!

Toastmasters members learn how to use the stage, body motion, gestures, hands, eyes, facial expressions, vocal variety, and even attire and props to deliver powerful speeches. They learn how to use the two ends of a stage to separate out two sides of an issue and then come to the center to discuss the resolution. They learn to avoid distracting jewelry, clothing, or name badges that might cause audience members to be distracted. Even a momentary drift can cause the audience to lose concentration and miss a portion of the speech.

Toastmasters leadership development programs include meeting roles for members to perform at each meeting. Club officers are elected annually. In addition, members serve as Area, Division, District, Regional, National, and global officers. Each new officer is supported and mentored by previous officers and members.

Toastmasters members develop and practice a wide range of speeches of varying lengths such as Table Topics, Humorous Speeches, Social Speeches such as acceptance speeches and eulogies, and even keynotes, panel moderation and professional podcasts.

Table Topics speeches help members learn to talk impromptu on any topic for one to two minutes. This skill is extremely helpful for speakers to practice responding to audience questions. Humorous speeches help speakers to inject fun and laughter into speeches and generate engagement and impact.

Toastmasters members also practice listening skills; they learn to summarize key points made by a speaker and provide actionable feedback, which speakers use to improve their speeches. Toastmasters clubs also host multiple speech contests so speakers can take their speechcraft to exceptionally high levels. Toastmasters organizations encourage members to use technology, so they are comfortable in both online and in person events. Toastmasters meetings are timed, and members and clubs are rewarded for meeting and maintaining high standards.

Most Toastmasters clubs develop symbiotic relationships with their local chambers of commerce and other community organizations, which create valuable networking and speaking opportunities for members. Toastmasters members frequently receive professional speaking invitations and opportunities to conduct paid workshops. Finally, as a new member explained, "Toastmasters is a great place to stay connected with people, develop friendships, and enjoy camaraderie; it is far cheaper than a therapist."

This organization is such a powerful and affordable forum for leadership development that many companies provide facilities and pay the nominal membership fees for their employees to belong to company sponsored clubs. I was a member of such a club from 1991 to 1994.

I rejoined in 2019 and I am having the time of my life leveling up my leadership and public speaking skills and experimenting with new ideas. I am also enjoying mentoring and coaching several new members; all are making amazing speeches and progressing rapidly. They are also observing, evaluating, and learning from each other.

The genesis for the title of this book happened over a series of Toastmasters meetings. First, our District told us that our slogan for this year will be *Level Up*. Based on that, as President, I decided to make a short Invocation speech at my first meeting titled *Bring Inner Greatness Out*. Soon this slogan was adopted by our club membership.

At the following meeting, a new member cited my Invocation speech and shared how she had internalized the idea that greatness is a choice in a remarkable speech! A few weeks later, I decided to make a longer speech at another club about Personal Brand expanding on the idea. While preparing the club speech, I suddenly remembered that I had already done an outline for this book based on my Personal Branding workshops.

It was time to complete this book - the inspirational spark had happened! I realized *Bring Inner Greatness Out* would make a perfect title for the book. *Personal Brand* could be the subtitle. I quickly started working on a cover design and floated a few cover designs and the proposed title of this book with my professional network as well as my Toastmasters club.

The trustworthy and valuable feedback from the club speech assured me I was on the right track. Anyone with the desire to become a high quality professional public speaker should spend at least one year with Toastmasters. Join one or more Toastmasters clubs and you will find that your journey to greatness will be simplified and accelerated dramatically!

5.3 EMBRACE DISCOMFORT AS THE FIRST STEP TO GREATNESS

Discomfort is natural anytime you do something you have never done before. However, discomfort is also the first sign that you are enhancing brain prowess and acquiring new skills. Your embrace of discomfort will help you recalibrate your shyness and introversion and give you more confidence.

Doing familiar things may seem easy. However, that is also a recipe for stagnation. Every time you do something that makes you uncomfortable, you are working towards greatness.

The human brain is just like a muscle. There are entire bodies of literature around neurogenesis and neuroplasticity that share the science behind the brain's ability to develop continuously. Neurogenesis is the brain's ability to grow new neurons, while neuroplasticity is the brain's ability to reconfigure, connect, and reorganize neural networks.

At first a new idea or the acquisition of new knowledge and skills may cause some discomfort. This is like exercising. Every time you use a new muscle or start a new exercise routine, your body will ache. However, that ache is the first sign that the exercise is working. This is true of the brain as well; it becomes easier over time.

Every time you do a new thing or try a new challenge, your brain will develop further, and you will bring out more of your greatness. Since we are all chemical beings, every success will beget more success because every success will release good chemicals in your body. These good chemicals will allow your brain to function at a higher capacity. On the contrary, spending time and energy within a negative or stressful situation will release bad chemicals, which will be harmful to your health. Stress and hostile environments are known to reduce human productivity and innovation dramatically.

5.4 EMBRACE GREATNESS AS A PRACTICED ART

Like riding a bicycle or learning to drive a car, practice is the only way to improve. You cannot be a good driver by just reading books. As you discover and embrace yourself and start to celebrate who you are and what you have, instead of lamenting what you do not have, this way of thinking will become second nature to you. You will gain control of your destiny, your income, and your outcomes!

It certainly happened for me. This is how I survived every layoff. I never blamed myself since there was nothing to blame myself for; instead, I believed in myself! A layoff speaks far more about the broken nature of an organization and its executive leaders than it does about the people who are laid off. In most cases, people conducting the layoffs do not have a strong understanding of what it takes to run the organization. Nor do they understand who the money makers are.

Mass layoffs and across the board reductions and furloughs are a clear sign of weak leadership and a failure to make difficult strategic choices. It shows that the leadership is working from a spreadsheet and doing the simple thing. Layoffs are often done by brand new top level executives brought in from the outside with little or no understanding, history, or relationship with the organization; a cost reduction on paper may help them demonstrate quick results.

However, mass layoffs and across the board cuts always result in greater long term revenue loss compared to the short term expenses reduced. Sometimes, the entire short term savings are offset by the expenses of the layoff itself! Taking a strategic approach to make surgical changes would require more thinking, learning, and analysis, and may result in no revenue loss at all.

Most often, the best way to address a financial shortfall is to create alternative revenue opportunities. My own confidence in the value of my work and my personal brand always provided a soft landing for the layoffs I faced. According to my observations, the financial losses to the organizations that conducted layoffs were astronomical compared to any temporary financial setback I experienced.

In every case, the reputation loss for the organizations was tragic! Academic program reputations built over a long period of time were lost in an instant!

5.4.1 Be Stronger than Organizational Brands

Technology has democratized the power of mass communications. While organizations used to wield tremendous power in the world of expensive traditional media such as TV, radio, and newspapers, individuals now wield power in the new world of free and low cost social media.

Organizational brands have suffered a dramatic decline in brand affinity during the last forty years because of their ignominious history of mistreating people by reducing benefits and job security. This has directly resulted in reducing employee allegiance and loyalty. Furthermore, it is far more natural for people to bond with other people.

In social media, people rarely interact with nameless, faceless companies. They are far more likely to bond with other people. Therefore, people can become strong brand representatives for organizations simply through the sheer power of their personal brands.

I discovered this in 2017 when I competed in several voting contests against companies with large marketing budgets and large databases of employees and customers. I found that a personal connection is a far greater motivator for voting than an organizational affiliation. People develop emotional connections with people; people vote for people.

5.5 BECOME CHARISMATIC

No one is born with charisma. Charisma is bestowed upon us by people who benefit from our contributions, believe in what we share, and wish to join our circle of influence. Therefore, revealing more of ourselves, sharing our greatness, teaching others what we know, and mentoring others are the surest ways for us to become charismatic.

This is also the essence of leadership. Therefore, to become charismatic, share experiences and lessons from your life. Only you know this story and can share it best. Take your listeners through the same emotional journey you went through and then help them vicariously overcome the adversity as you did. Connect with people on an emotional level and you will have lasting relationships and impact.

I have shared positive and negative stories of my life countless times in interviews, speeches, and conversations because I wanted to make sure everyone realizes that good and bad events are a normal part of life. Such revealing stories as the one in the Information Governance World Magazine are critical in showing others how we are just like any other human being - with some flaws - but with the ability to solve the problems life throws our way: https://infogovworld.com/ig-topics/an-interview-with-dr-mansur-hasib-cybersecurity-leader/

Complainers are useless. Problem solvers are valuable. Help others become successful. Help them solve problems. In doing so, you will find you know more about solving problems than you ever realized. Your message will also begin to crystallize and become sharper and clearer. As people learn more about you and your talents, and as they engage with your positive energy, they will bestow charisma upon you; that is how you will become charismatic.

The key ingredients powering your charisma will be your knowledge and your people network; they are all interrelated. Some of my networking tips are shared later in the book. As you share your knowledge, your people network will grow. Your knowledge will also increase as you engage with other knowledgeable people in your network. *Your network determines your net worth!*

5.6 PROTECT THE VALUE OF YOUR PERSONAL BRAND

The value of your personal brand is fluid. It can increase and decrease based on your activities. Stay in your lane. Straying from your primary purposes into areas outside your area of expertise or mission can hurt your personal brand. It can also shrink your market.

Such brand dilution commonly happens to actors and singers when they stray from their primary mission of artistic endeavors to politics or religion. Even though they may help the political or religious cause, they will invariably divide their market. Each person must decide if the benefits of such deviations are worth the costs; sometimes they are.

Your personal brand value can also be affected by the activities of others. In most cases, your supporters will help to enhance the value of your personal brand. However, you will have plenty of naysayers - some will think you are insane. You may even suffer from an imposter syndrome and think you are not good enough. Surround yourself with yea-sayers to inoculate yourself. Everyone has knowledge, skills, and abilities others do not have. Your personality itself is an asset.

Listen to credible trustworthy people giving you constructive advice. Watch out for people who only point out flaws but never offer possible ways for you to solve them. Be wary of people who criticize physical attributes or similar things you cannot change. If someone only notices your weaknesses and never notices your strengths, that person is not a credible source. If someone does not offer a constructive solution to a problem they point out in you, be careful; *their primary purpose may be to cut you down and not to build you up.*

People who wish to cause damage to your personal brand may use falsehoods and rumors to cause harm. In the current electronic age, just as you need to be vigilant of your own activities, you need to stay vigilant of potentially damaging activities by others and take appropriate action, which may include complaints, cease and desist orders, or the engagement of law enforcement. Even social media giants are finally waking up to their responsibility in preventing false information from spreading.

CHAPTER 6

Step by Step Process

Now that you are armed with a good understanding of a personal brand, why you need it, and how to build it, let us go through the step by step process of defining and building your personal brand.

6.1 CHOOSE YOUR NAME

Your first decision will be to choose your name. If this surprises you, ask yourself if you have variations of your name floating around. You were given a legal name. Do you prefer to use some variation of it? Do you prefer a particular spelling or pronunciation?

Do you have a nickname? Do you go by different names in different circles? Do you like degrees, certifications, rank, or honorifics to accompany your name? If so, in what order, and why? Do you have a doctoral degree or are you a medical doctor? If so, do you wish to put the Dr. in front of your name or a degree after your name?

I recommend putting the Dr. in front of your name and not the degree afterwards because most people will think it is a certification. This will diminish the value of your degree and your personal brand - specially if you have some certifications listed after your name also.

I know one person who had a PhD after her name for 20 years. At my suggestion, she put the Dr. in front of her name. Suddenly, people took notice; the impact was instantaneous. Most people in her circles had no idea she had a doctoral degree.

Someone else had a complex first name and a preferred nickname both listed. I suggested dropping the unused legal first name and simply listing the nickname. Once again the positive impact was immediate.

If you prefer to be called something, why even display something else? Make it simple for others. Your name and the way you choose to display it, is the beginning of your personal brand.

As you achieve your greatness and become famous, your name will grow in recognition and value. Therefore, consistency of display is key. Every time you change the display of your name, you will have to start all over again with the development of your new personal brand.

This is like a company becoming famous under a certain brand name and then deciding to change it. Too many companies make the error of discarding or changing a brand name after decades of building brand value into the name. These companies choose a new name only to find out that the new name immediately detracts from the value of the brand - simply because of reduced name recognition.

Brand names can also connote quality or appeal to a particular type of clientele. When the company name is changed, it may no longer appeal to the same clientele. Once a brand is damaged due to a name change, it is exceedingly difficult to recover.

Your name is no different. You must consciously choose the name you want to become famous in. After your chosen name increases in brand value, do not change it. Every time you change it, your previous investments in building your personal brand are lost.

Do you typically like to go by your middle name? If so, is there any reason to mention the first name or initial? Do you typically like to go by your initials? If you have a middle name, you will need to make a conscious decision what to do with it; decide if you wish to use your middle name, middle initial, or drop it altogether. Make it easy for your name to become a verb or an adjective some day!

What about your last name? Do you intend to change your last name if your marital status changes? Do you wish to maintain anonymity and use a pen name or a stage name? The key is to understand that your personal brand name can be completely different from your legal name.

Suppose your legal first name is Richard, but you like to go by Dick or Rick or Rich. You should decide which variation of your name will be your personal brand name. Thoughtful choices will help you develop a strong personal brand sooner - specially if your personal brand name is simple and catchy compared to your legal name.

Names that are different from your legal name can have the side benefit of giving you some level of anonymity, privacy, or even protection from identity theft. Many people become famous in names other than their legal names. Sometimes they adopt a name with no relationship with their legal name.

In choosing a personal brand name, always remember that while there may be some level of personal satisfaction in choosing your legal name, the primary goal of any personal brand is to appeal to others - just like a company name. Think from a marketing perspective. Your primary goal is to create brand affinity with your name.

So, choose the name you wish to become famous in and stick with it. I chose Dr. Mansur Hasib as the consistent way to display my name. I adorn it with the CISSP, PMP, and CPHIMS certifications.

CISSP is an internationally well-known and respected certification in cybersecurity. PMP is an internationally recognized certification in project management, and CPHIMS is well respected as a healthcare certification. Each of these elements conveys meaning to the public without any words being spoken.

After choosing your name, systematically do all items in the following figure, which are also explained in detail below:

HOW DO WE BUILD A PERSONAL BRAND?

Narrow Focus on Key Passion
Stay In Your Lane
Choose A Symbol
Concentrate On Being The Best At Something
Focus Everything Around Your Passion

How Do We Build a Personal Brand?

6.2 FOCUS ON KEY PASSION

The key is to focus keenly on a passion that supports your personal mission and ensures that all your efforts will surround this passion. Your actions, words, presentations, and writings must focus on this passion. Whatever it may be, you must concentrate on being the best in the world at it. You can choose a niche and focus on acquiring a unique set of qualifications that distinguishes you from anyone else.

Consciously embrace a set of values and be true to your values as you pursue your passion. Your values will define who you are and will guide your behavior. Live your values; project your values in your work and share stories about how you acquired them and why you chose them.

Values form the barometer that will govern your behavior. People like authentic people. Your values should be reflected in everything you do. You should not engage in activities that will compromise your values.

6.2.1 Content Marketing

You need to acquire a significant amount of knowledge in your area of passion and share enough of this knowledge so that it benefits others; helps others succeed. Share with the idea of educating others.

The content you share must be useful to others. That is the key to content marketing. In doing so, you will become known as the expert in your area of passion. If there is no one else doing what you are doing, you will become known amazingly fast!

I call this concept playing the game no one else is playing. If you create your own game, and you are the only player, you are automatically the champion. Do not play someone else's game that is already rigged against you? Instead, change the game.

The only way to win in a rigged game is to change the game! If others catch up with you, change the game again! If you keep changing the game, no one can ever catch up with you!

The knowledge you share does not have to be your original knowledge. You can share links, synthesize, summarize, and review the works of others (with proper citation of course). Book reviews are an excellent way to share other people's works in a value added manner.

You can publish these reviews online in a wide range of forums. The authors of the books you reviewed may share your reviews around or comment on them. Now you will get cross brand promotion!

I do not recommend locking your work away in commercial journals unless you are getting paid for them. You will gain more views in open online forums. Do not be shy about putting your content out in a wide range of forums.

You can also repost them with a comment or two every now and then. Since you will need to share content with some level of regularity, always feel free to repost something. Content frequency is far more important than content length.

Content marketing is not the same thing as selling. As a matter of fact, the selling part is very subtle. If all your content is about buying your products and services or the products and services of your company, you will lose personal brand affinity real fast. You must share knowledge. You must give value to your network!

You must also engage in the content marketing posts from your network. A relationship is a two way street. As you engage with others, others will engage with you. This is the best way to develop cross brand promotional relationships with other influencers in your network. Soon others will reshare or call attention to your posts. Such resharing is powerful.

Even a Like is great. Comments are even better. If someone comments on your post, respond to the comment - at least with a Like. The more you acknowledge the engagement from your network, the more engagement you will receive.

Even though you are using technology to maintain relationships on a large scale, always remember that you have a human being with feelings on the other side. Be sensitive to feelings. Be respectful of others - even if you disagree.

6.2.2 Frequency vs Content Length

Frequency of engagement and content marketing is far more important than the length of the content. For example, five one-minute videos can have a much larger impact compared to one five-minute video. Sharing five one-minute videos over a period of five days is much better than sharing all of them in one day.

Similarly, spend a small amount of time engaging every day instead of spending a large chunk of time once a week or once a month. Think of it like a relationship with someone you love. Wouldn't you prefer to hear, "I love you" once every day for a month instead of hearing it thirty times on one day of every month?

Social media content marketing is all about relationships. Sales of your services and products will happen as a natural byproduct of your relationships with countless people. The more relationships you can develop and maintain, the more sales you will generate - without ever placing ads or promotional posts. Pure promotional posts in social media are a major turn off. The stronger your personal brand, the more sales you will generate!

Choose commonly available digital tools and social media to network and promote your brand. Amazingly enough, most of the platforms you can use to build and promote your brand are free. LinkedIn,

Facebook, Twitter, Instagram are all examples of powerful free personal brand building platforms.

6.3 STAY IN YOUR LANE

Your passion and mission define your focus. Your clarity of purpose must be salient in all your professional efforts. If you deviate from this focus by straying into topics that are outside your expertise or mission, you will dilute your personal brand and soften your chances of success in achieving your primary goals.

Some clear examples of such deviation are political or religious activism by actors or musicians. While it is completely appropriate to participate in voting or religion privately, activities denouncing other views are bound to cause a bifurcation of their fan base. Such bifurcation will cause them to lose fans and associated revenue.

When you discuss issues outside your areas of expertise, people may wonder about your expertise in all areas. For example, if you are not a healthcare professional, does it make sense for you to be talking about the subject? Doing so will diminish the impact of your message in your core subject areas.

6.4 CHOOSE A SYMBOL

Just like a company chooses a brand symbol and a logo to represent its brand, you should choose a symbol or a logo to represent your personal brand. Pictures are powerful and can convey a lot of meaning without the use of any words.

You may need to experiment before you settle on something that sticks and becomes powerful. In my case, my choice of the crested giant saguaro to symbolize leadership and to reflect my own personal brand has been amazing. It has generated curiosity and questions and many conversations. These conversations were the beginnings of relationships with people. However, it took me a while to think of a symbol and settle on it.

6.5 CONCENTRATE ON BEING BEST AT SOMETHING

Being the best requires a significant level of humility to know that when you start your journey in a particular lane, you are unlikely to know all the issues or even most of the issues in that space. You are also unlikely to know the flaws in your thinking or the counter arguments to the likely challenges to your thinking. However, you must believe you can be the best in the world at something!

You must be willing to refine your thinking as you learn new issues relevant to your passion that you had not thought about before. You also need to develop well thought out responses to challenges and commonly asked questions. Sometimes you will need to adopt new words and definitions that capture your refined thinking and accommodate more people.

For example, in my case, between 2014 and 2017, I adapted the original definition of the word cybersecurity after visiting many conferences and peer reviewing my work with people in related disciplines. The final definition I settled on includes more aspects of the discipline and caters to all aspects of the cybersecurity model far better than the original definition I had published. The final definition was better received at multiple major scholarly and business conferences.

If you choose your niche carefully and focus on something that no one else is doing, you will be amazed at how rapidly you become recognized as the most knowledgeable person. In addition, even if more knowledgeable people exist, if they are not sharing their ideas or promoting their brands, you will have no competition and will easily rise to the top.

I have always approached any job or assignment with the mindset that I will be the best in the world in that job or assignment. You will find that if you approach anything with this mindset, it will become a self-fulfilling prophecy. You will find yourself innovating in that role like no one else can. You will have fun and the challenge will be inspiring! Through your continuous refinements you will soon achieve your goal of being the best in the world.

6.6 FOCUS EVERYTHING AROUND YOUR PASSION

Once you have chosen your key passion, embraced a symbol, and carefully selected your lane, all your professional activities must revolve around this passion. Such consistency and focus will create highly positive results. You should also surround yourself with people who have symbiotic interests and related passions so they can amplify your voice and help you make strategic connections who will be important to your success. Many unsolicited and unadvertised opportunities will come from your people network.

 CYBERSECURITY DEFINITION

Cybersecurity is the mission-focused and risk-optimized governance of information, which maximizes confidentiality, integrity, and availability using a balanced mix of people, policy, and technology, while perennially improving over time.

-Dr. Mansur Hasib (2017)
Cybersecurity Leadership: Powering the Modern Organization
www.cybersecurityleadership.com

Example of a Widely Shared Slide Around My Passion

CHAPTER 7

Discovering My Personal Brand

While I have personally applied all the elements I have shared with you in the previous sections of this book, initially, I did not do so consciously. I was simply pursuing my passion and trying to help as many people as I possibly could. I was sharing my knowledge through university courses and degree programs, writings, books, conference presentations, and business social media. I did not fully understand what a personal brand is or how to build one.

I had heard of the word. I had heard people say everyone needs to have a personal brand. I could recognize people with strong personal brands. However, most appeared to have acquired this by serving in some high level position; their personal brands seemed intimately tied to having served in some role that carried a lot of authority, responsibility, or celebrity. So, the concept of anyone being able to develop a compelling personal brand was unknown to me.

As I continued to share my knowledge, I began to recognize marketing power in my voice. People viewed the programs I ran or the courses I taught very favorably, and they sent their friends to my classes and my programs. Any organization or program I was affiliated with appeared to gain credibility.

I noticed people made an effort to attend events once they heard I was speaking. They told their friends to attend. I met people who flew from the West Coast to the East Coast or took the train from Boston to Baltimore to hear me speak at a conference and to get their copy of my book Cybersecurity Leadership autographed. People wanted to take pictures with me; they wanted to thank me for promotions they received or new jobs they obtained by using ideas from my book.

I started to understand personal branding!

7.1   2017 PEOPLE'S CHOICE AWARD IN CYBERSECURITY

On March 22, 2017, I stunned myself and every company in the contest by winning the coveted People's Choice Award (decided by global public voting) in the first ever Maryland Cybersecurity Awards. There were twenty three contenders - four individuals and nineteen companies. All contenders were finalists in various categories of awards and were entered into the voting for this award and anyone from anywhere could vote for one of the contenders.

There were publicity and media companies as well as large companies with over a million subscribers, hefty marketing budgets, and massive databases of email addresses to contact for voting purposes. My budget for marketing was $0 and my database of contacts for voter outreach was under 5,000; my work was not well known globally yet.

As the votes started coming in each day, the executives of the large companies were puzzled. They had not seen anything similar before. They wondered how an individual could garner so many votes! How could an academic faculty member or Program Chair? However, everyone else had a blast watching an underdog win!

During the entire experience, I observed a fascinating phenomenon. Even though my primary database of people was small, when my global supporters learned that I was a contender, they mobilized to support me in a way I had never seen before. They solicited their networks to vote for me; people I did not know voted simply because their friends or relatives had asked them.

It was fascinating and heartwarming for me to watch faculty members, students, former students, and professional colleagues all over the world campaign on my behalf through blogs, stories, articles, phone calls, email, and social media to vote for me. My first degree connections had mobilized their own connections and people who had simply heard my name through my work cast votes on my behalf and even sent me messages wishing me the best.

My students were particularly passionate about campaigning! Many got their children, family members, and friends to vote and then excitedly told me how many votes they had been able to get. My niece threatened to unfriend people if they did not vote for me! Thus, my network of 5,000 people turned out to be huge with this amazing network multiplier effect!

This type of passionate mobilization is almost never seen on behalf of a company! People do not have a strong emotional attachment to company brands anymore. It is extremely hard for someone to get their family members, relatives, or friends to vote for a nameless faceless company - even if they work for that company. The fact that people affiliate with people and not with companies started to get crystallized in my brain.

 MULTIPLE AWARDS 2017 THROUGH 2020

Global Online Voting
Competing Against Multi-Billion Dollar Companies
Sales and Marketing Dramatically Changed
Ads Expensive, Low Impact, Short Shelf Life
Personal Brand, Low Cost, High Impact, Long Shelf Life
Content and Personal Brand Marketing Rules
Knowledge Sharing Rules

Multiple Awards 2017 through 2020

When I posted the picture of my win on social media, the post received more than 20,000 views and hundreds of Likes, Comments, and Shares within two days. I could see that in the modern world, once a connection through technology has been made, people connect with people in a far more powerful way than they ever connect with an organization. When people vote, they are voting for the person; most of the time they are not conscious of the organization.

For people to vote for an organization, that organization must be front-ended by someone with a strong personal brand! I would never vote blindly for an organization. However, if I respected and cared about someone or knew someone close to me who had been helped by someone in the contest, I would be inspired to vote for the person.

I took an early lead in the Maryland contest during the very first week and never relinquished the lead. Companies that had expected to win and even the organizers were just as surprised at the phenomenon as I was. Most rooted for me as I was viewed as the underdog and most unlikely to win against so many companies. The win sealed the incredible power and potential of a personal brand in me forever!

Cybersecurity Association of Maryland, Inc. People's Choice Award

I did not win because of the organization I was affiliated with. In fact, most of the people who voted had no idea what organization I was representing. At that time, while I was employed full-time at UMUC, I was also teaching for other universities. All organizations I was affiliated with, were able to take advantage of the marketing benefits of my win and did so through stories and press releases.

I noted that my students and former students from UMBC voted for me instead of voting for someone from UMBC who was also contending that year. Thus, the power of my personal brand was overshadowing the power of the organizational brand even for students at a different university!

I had been teaching my students that technology had leveled the playing field in marketing, allowing individuals to build a compelling global personal brand. However, until this experience, I did not realize that such a personal brand could contend effectively against organizational brands.

7.2   2017 (ISC)² INFORMATION SECURITY LEADERSHIP AWARD

To my greatest surprise, the People's Choice Award in the global voting contest hosted by the Cybersecurity Association of Maryland, Inc. was the first of many awards to follow.

During 2017, my colleague Ajay Gupta nominated me for the 2017 (ISC)² Information Security Leadership Award for designing and implementing the competency-based Master of Science in Cybersecurity Technology program at UMUC in the Fall of 2016. Even though I had been nominated for this award in the past, he felt I had a better chance this year because of the groundbreaking nature of the project.

He had observed how this program featured small scale versions of real world projects our graduates would have to complete. We had eliminated textbooks with free high quality curated digital learning materials, built globally available cloud-based labs, recruited and retrained faculty members to teach in this innovative program using enhanced feedback and coaching techniques. We had partnered with Career Services to help students and graduates meet and talk with employers.

We had opened the program to anyone who wished to study in the program and worked extremely hard to provide each student with what they needed. He saw that the key strength of the program was in helping everyone succeed; students were not left to submit work one time and be judged on that initial attempt. Instead, they were judged on their ability to succeed in completing the project and gain the competency regardless of where they started or how many attempts they needed.

Ajay Gupta was right. His submission did catch the eye of the panel of global judges for the 2017 Information Security Leadership Award and I won the award on October 26, 2017. It was fitting that Ajay Gupta himself was my representative to receive the (ISC)^2 ISLA award and partake in all the festivities that evening as I had accepted an invitation to be at Providence, Rhode Island that same evening!

Since this award was tied to launching the new Master of Science in Cybersecurity Technology program, it made the program an award winning program - and it turned out to be an amazing draw to bring in students. Enrollment data showed a dramatic 48% increase in enrollment the following year - all while the rest of the graduate programs were seeing a decline of 4.2%!

7.3   2017 INFORMATION GOVERNANCE EXPERT OF THE YEAR

While I was a finalist for the (ISC)^2 award, on October 26, 2017, I was already invited to attend #INFOGOV17 to receive the 2017 Information Governance Expert of the Year Award with a final global vote tally of 2,256 votes. So, I chose to attend the awards ceremony for a certain win to benefit from the associated personal brand marketing benefits.

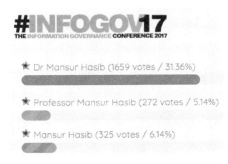

Final Vote Tally - 2017 INFOGOV Expert of the Year Award

In this globally contested event several interesting things happened. First, organizers allowed write-in voting in addition to the slate of nominated candidates for the award. Many of my voters did not note my name in the list or were confused about the voting process and wrote in my name as Professor Mansur Hasib. Some wrote in Mansur Hasib. After that, other people started to vote on whichever name they saw first. There was even one completely mangled entry with four votes that had to be discarded.

Second, after people noted the other names they wondered if their votes would be wasted. Some were worried that I was not leading in the contest when in fact I led in the contest throughout. So, they asked questions both publicly and privately. This worked in my favor because it led to more circulation of the contest, more questions, engagement, and comments, and more votes.

Finally, in any contest, the entire campaign period is an excellent opportunity for personal brand promotion and relationship building. This contest lasted for months and the final date for the results got pushed back several times. In addition to my own marketing and campaigning, my students, and global supporters campaigned heavily also.

The conference organizers also posted messages like the following for all contestants. These acted like earned media marketing. The prolonged contest was grueling. However, the exposure and marketing value of the contest was incredible for me personally as well as the institution I was affiliated with at that time.

As part of the festivities, I enjoyed a wonderful dinner, delivered a keynote, participated in a panel, played duckpin bowling at a historical place, and enjoyed an awesome awards event! The organizers marketed the contest and my win throughout the entire

InfoGovCon @InfoGovCon · Aug 7, 2017
Will Dr. Mansur Hasib (@mhasib) be named #InfoGov Expert of the Year 2017? Vote now: infogovcon.com/awards/vote-in... #InfoGov17

Earned Media Post by @InfoGovCon

time of the contest and for several weeks afterwards. As they promoted me, they also benefited from my own promotion and it was an excellent example of cross brand promotion with massive benefits for everyone at no cost!

#InfoGov Awards @InfoGovAwards · Mar 8, 2018   · · ·

Dr. **Mansur Hasib** (@MHasib) won "#InfoGov Expert of the Year 2017". Who will win this year? You choose. infogovcon.com/awards/

With Nick Inglis and #InfoGov17 Expert of the Year Award

#InfoGov Expert of the Year

2017: Dr. Mansur Hasib

#InfoGov Expert of the Year 2017: Dr. Mansur Hasib

Marketing photographs must tell a story instead of simply being a formal professional shot. The more intrigue the photograph conveys, the more likely it is to generate questions and conversations. For example, after I won the $(ISC)^2$ Americas Information Security Leadership award in 2017, I posed with the award guitar for several photos and one came out amazing!

With the 2017 (ISC)2 ISLA Americas Award Electric Guitar

The number of questions and intrigue this picture has generated is incalculable.

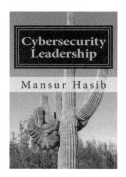

**Cover of
Cybersecurity
Leadership: Powering
the Modern
Organization**

Similarly, the picture of the Giant Crested Saguaro on the cover of my book Cybersecurity Leadership has become synonymous with me and that book!

CHAPTER 8

Developing My Personal Brand

Once I recognized what had happened, I realized others could benefit from my methodology and experiences. So, I prepared several presentations and workshops on Personal Branding and began to share some of the ideas shared in this book. We also made personal branding a key concept taught in my graduate program and my short 35 minute video of the key concepts was adopted as a key learning resource for all incoming students of the graduate school.

8.1 MY LEADERSHIP MISSION: HELP PEOPLE SUCCEED

My narrow focus in life has always been to help others succeed. I enjoy people, and I enjoy finding out more about them, and I enjoy having lots of friends. My leadership and behavior are shaped by several key values that I have consciously embraced.

MY MISSION IN LIFE: HELP PEOPLE SUCCEED

Behavior Shaped By Values:

Integrity
Empowerment
Teamwork
Customer Service
Continuous Improvement
Positive Reinforcement

My Mission in Life: Help People Succeed

8.2 MY VALUES

In my book Cybersecurity Leadership: Powering the Modern Organization, I wrote how my values guided my behavior. Values can not only guide the behavior of people; it can also form the culture of organizations. Organizations with value driven culture benefit from the collective brainpower of all its members instead of the brainpower of a few anointed leaders.

Selecting values is fundamental to the development of a personal brand. Think of your values as the barometer that drives your individual culture of behavior. Values guide our decision-making; they help us decide between right and wrong. Values make us human. Values prevent us from engaging in or supporting criminal behavior.

Values also help us determine the difference between ethical and unethical behavior. We must think, act, and live in accordance with our values. Others need to be able to trust that we will act in accordance with our values. There must not be any difference between our expressed values and our practiced values.

Values are important because we cannot always rely upon the law to be fair and ethical. Historically, laws have frequently been used to justify unethical and oppressive behavior. For example, slavery was legal in the

US and voting rights for women and other groups were suppressed for more than a hundred years.

Just because something is legal does not mean it is ethical. Our barometer of values helps us to create better alignment between legal and ethical activities. This barometer controls the brain chemicals that guide our behavior. If integrity is a value for us, we will have a terrible chemical reaction if we lie. We may have knots in our stomach if we engage in criminal behavior.

On the contrary when we act according to our values, our brain should release good chemicals to give us a sense of satisfaction. However, prolonged normalization of unethical and illegal activities can alter the internal barometer such that the unethical or illegal activities start to give us far more pleasure than ethical or legal activities.

This is the key reason we must have harmony between what we say and what we do. Humans can become comfortable with lying. They can say one thing and do something completely contrary to what they are saying. Unfortunately, the laws governing lying are typically weak across the world. Lying by politicians is accepted as normal. Such normalization is dangerous for society.

Thus, it is important for us as individuals to lead by example and demand others do what they say. We should not condone unethical behavior in our personal and professional lives. Once again, the stronger our personal brands, the stronger our voices to lead by example. As more ethical people decide to take control of their incomes and outcomes, widespread change for the good will become more likely.

My chosen set of leadership values are integrity, empowerment, teamwork, customer service, continuous learning, and positive reinforcement. These values have guided my behavior and have been the barometer that guided the behavior of all organizations I led.

People working on my teams were required to adhere to these values; their actions had to be congruent with these values. We discussed values in team meetings and each person had to discuss what each value meant to them and how they planned to operationalize them in their behavior.

We discussed actions and made decisions with complete consciousness of the values that guided us.

How many values we choose is less important than taking the conscious step to choose some values. We can have two or three values or a set of six or seven. However, a limited set of broad values typically works better. As with anything, constant practice, regular discussions, and tabletop exercises and drills will help us to make this habitual.

8.2.1 Integrity

Integrity is doing the right thing when no one is looking. Integrity takes a lifetime to achieve but can be lost in a moment. Integrity requires people to always work in the best interests of the organization and the community they serve. People of integrity are committed to their jobs, work with minimal supervision and take pride in what they do.

8.2.2 Empowerment

Empowerment allows key decisions to be made by the person most qualified to make the decision – usually at the lowest possible level of the organization rather than at the highest. Thus, decisions are made by people closest to the problem and with the best understanding of the issue. This value unleashes powerful levels of productivity, energy, and innovation within an organization because people feel that they matter. Empowerment fosters self-confidence and the organization solves more problems simultaneously. It reduces more risks in an organization because everyone is engaged in assessing the risk of each action with a questioning attitude. People are not penalized for questioning orders if they believe the orders diminish the safety of the organization.

8.2.3 Teamwork

Teamwork is the magic potion which allows ordinary people to achieve extraordinary results. Good teams have diverse skills, and each member is a leader and an expert in something. Members lead in some aspect and follow in other aspects. They know each other's strengths and understand how each role contributes to the success of the organization.

Team members hone their leadership skills within the trusted environment of the team. Instead of competing against each other, competition is defined as each member trying to do better each day compared to how they performed in the past. Frank and free discussions and constructive criticism is encouraged, and each innovative idea is refined until a team decision with the best mitigation of risk is reached.

8.2.4 Customer Service

Happy customers ensure demand for services, which translates into job security. Customer requirements are understood clearly by asking probing questions. Even if someone asks for a product, we must learn the business purpose to ensure that we meet that purpose. Given limited resources, we must negotiate realistic expectations, including the scope and delivery schedule for the request. We must explain and promptly rectify any unplanned deviations from an agreement.

8.2.5 Continuous Improvement

Quality improvement is automatic when every person in an organization focuses on continuous improvement and demonstrates a willingness to take calculated risks with innovative ideas. A reasonable portion of the organization's resources must be spent on research and innovation. Continuous improvement is another key to job security because it spurs innovation and obviates obsolescence. Within the protected environment of the team, members learn new skills often by partnering with experienced members. They learn with a questioning attitude and a fresh set of eyes, always looking for ways to improve the process.

8.2.6 Positive Reinforcement

Positive reinforcement creates an environment where people enjoy coming to work because they feel their work is valuable. They build symbiotic relationships with others and develop a sense of loyalty to the organization. Having fun at work is important. When people enjoy work, they are more productive. Positive reinforcement is best created with non-monetary rewards.

Though we have a limited supply of monetary rewards, we have an unlimited supply of non-monetary rewards. We must celebrate not just successes; we need to celebrate, discuss, and learn from innovative failures. Absence of such a culture will stifle risk taking and innovation.

8.3 MY PERSONAL BRAND SYMBOL: THE GIANT CRESTED SAGUARO

Initially, I did not go out seeking a personal brand symbol; I did not develop awareness of this concept until mass media communications became available to all individuals. Over the years, I did experiment with various symbols on my business cards; they were mostly decorative.

In 2014, after I completed the journey of writing Cybersecurity Leadership where I shared my core values and experiences as an organizational leader for over thirty years, I decided to find a symbol for the cover of the book. I wanted a symbol that not only embraced all my values but also connoted a higher purpose for me to strive for. I wanted a symbol that would generate questions, start conversations, and express meaning without any words being spoken.

As I went through my collection of photographs I had taken, I recalled my visit to the Desert Botanical Garden, in Phoenix, Arizona, USA on December 9, 2012. I was fascinated by the story of the lone Giant Crested Saguaro in the garden. The tour guide shared legends about these Giant Saguaros in general and explained the rarity of the Giant Crested Saguaros.

I became consumed by the traits of these magnificent trees; the legendary lore of how people have personified and revered them for thousands of years overwhelmed me. I began to see clearly how this Giant Crested Saguaro personified all the traits I value. As I have explained below, I also appreciated the alignment of these traits with my own set of chosen values.

MY BRAND SYMBOL: THE GIANT CRESTED SAGUARO

- **Leadership**
- **Teamwork**
- **Hard Work**
- **Perseverance**
- **Focus on Problem Solution**
- **Humility**
- **Integrity in Purpose**
- **Continuous Improvement**
- **Harmonious Coexistence**

My Brand Symbol: The Giant Crested Saguaro

8.3.1 Leadership

When I came upon this graceful giant, I was awestruck. I spent a long time contemplating her sturdy beauty and grace. Although each giant saguaro is unique, I found this one to be clearly extra special. She had found a way to learn something and to do something which distinguishes her even further. She has developed a crest that no one else in that garden has!

Only one in about 200,000 Giant Saguaros will ever develop a crest. Though many theories abound, no one knows why this happens. This is the only crested giant saguaro in this garden. I felt that this Giant Crested Saguaro represents to me what leadership is all about.

8.3.2 Teamwork

Although this cactus lives in a forest with other distinguished giants – where every saguaro is unique and distinct in their own way – she has spread her shallow roots far and wide to quickly capture the little moisture that the sparse rainfalls bring each year. Her roots intertwine with the roots of all the other cacti around her; together they provide each other the stability and strength they all need to support their tall stature. What an example of teamwork!

8.3.3 Hard Work

She is not an ordinary cactus tree but a Giant Saguaro – a special breed of giant cacti found only in the southwestern part of the USA and parts of Mexico. The Saguaro National Forest near Tucson, Arizona is full of these amazing giants. Life for these cacti is difficult indeed!

8.3.4 Perseverance

She is likely to have developed to her current stature in more than a hundred years and she is likely to survive a few hundred more. She matured slowly and deliberately; her first arms appeared when she was about 50 to 60 years old. She believed in her ability to execute and she executed with endurance!

8.3.5 Focus on Problem Solution

Her surroundings are harsh, and her problems are many. The desert becomes extremely hot during the day and very chilly at night. She does not complain about her problems. She focuses on solutions instead of the problems. She stores water in her giant body and protects herself from deer and other animals with her sharp pointed thorns – just like everyone else. Thus, she endures for hundreds of years.

8.3.6 Humility

She is subtle about her crest. Though she expresses her leadership, she blends in humility among the hundreds of other giant saguaros around her. Many people will pass her by and never see her unique qualities unless they are careful enough to observe.

8.3.7 Integrity in Purpose

She flowers gracefully and bears fruit just like a dutiful member of her flock. She gives shelter to woodpeckers and other little birds just like everyone else. She silently endures the harsh dry desert conditions just like everyone around her. She remains true to her existential purpose.

8.3.8 Continuous Improvement

She is an inspiration for all other giant saguaros around her. She reaches for the sky tall and proud – and her elegant beauty is difficult to capture in a single photo frame. She grows taller every year, with larger flowers and more arms. She encourages everyone to develop a crest of their own and to do something more meaningful and larger than themselves. She wants everyone to develop a better version of themselves.

8.3.9 Harmonious Coexistence

She supports and motivates all the other cacti around her as well as the birds, insects, and bats to be better than they think they are capable of. She is not aggressive to anyone; she welcomes all except those who might seek to cause her harm. What a marvelous example of existing in harmony!

As I contemplated her awesome example of leadership and her embodiment of values, I felt that if I embraced her as the symbol of my personal brand and put her on the cover of my book about leadership, she would speak for me without words being exchanged; she would cause intrigue and spark questions! And, every question she inspired would facilitate conversations and lead to relationships - which is exactly the purpose of a personal brand symbol!

8.4 AN ANECDOTE

The impact of selecting the Giant Crested Saguaro as my personal brand symbol was immediate and dramatic on several levels. Not only did it spark several questions, conversations, and deeper discussions about personal branding, the atypical cover made the book appealing and non-threatening to non-cybersecurity professionals.

People are attracted to the book by the cover. Some ask, "Are you from Arizona?" "Is this book about Arizona?" Some share stories of their visits to Phoenix or Tucson. After they read the title, they ask, "What does this cactus have to do with cybersecurity?" These questions are priceless and exactly what I anticipated the cover would do.

First, I was able to explain that the book was not about cybersecurity but about cybersecurity leadership. Second, I explained why people and leadership are the foundation of cybersecurity. Third, I explained the difference between leadership and management.

Most importantly, I was able to explain my personal brand and ask if they had a personal brand or any interest is learning to define it. Often, these discussions led to a dramatic awakening by many. People started to think about their own personal brands.

During one recent conference, I stopped by a booth that did not appear busy, just to network with the vendor and to express my support for sponsoring the event. Of course, after he saw my business card, he asked about the cactus and told me he had been to Arizona and had seen similar cacti.

I then showed him my book and explained what that crested giant saguaro represented. Pretty soon we were chatting like old friends. I asked him if he had a personal brand. He excitedly told me, "Yes, I am known as the Kevin Bacon of cybersecurity!"

I looked at the plain business card he had handed me, and asked, "Have you thought about putting a picture of two pieces of bacon on your business card?" He understood immediately the impact such a picture would have! He told me he would put the picture on the back of his card.

I explained that I had experimented with that already. I suggested he put the picture on the front; the back of the card needs to be plain white and non-glossy so people can write on that side. Many people, including me, use the back of the business card to write notes about a conversation. This can be critical information for any follow up conversations!

8.5 BUILDING MY BRAND THROUGH KNOWLEDGE SHARING

Once I had clearly defined my personal focus, values, and brand symbol, I carefully crafted a plan to promote my personal brand and my work to enhance its value. As a digital strategist for most of my professional life, my analysis revealed several key changes in the modern world of marketing.

8.5.1 Democratization of Media

First, major social media platforms such as LinkedIn, Facebook, Twitter, Instagram, and YouTube have brought the power of mass communications to everyone. Everyone now has global reach and can share their message and content globally at zero or little cost.

Second, in the traditional world, mass media communications and advertising through radio, TV, and newspapers are only available to large organizations with massive marketing budgets. Technology companies must sponsor conferences and set up expensive booths to let the world know of their products. Smaller brands and individuals have no chance to get their messages out and are essentially squeezed out.

However, such expensive marketing and ads have a noticeably short shelf life. Thus, they must be repeated frequently; their impact has diminished dramatically in the modern world. Viewers find ways to bypass ads altogether and do not share ads with others. Furthermore, newspapers, radio, and TV are losing subscribers as people increasingly move to free internet based channels for almost all their media consumption.

On top of that, the cost of a social media post is zero, and its shelf life is permanent. If the message and content are useful, they are shared around by people in our network and promoted even further by the connections of the people in our network! Thus, a single post has the potential to reach thousands and even millions of views within minutes! The impact can be dramatic!

Similarly, *in the modern world of marketing, expensive TV, radio, and newspaper ads and expensive booths at conferences do not result in increased student enrollment - particularly at the graduate level since a large proportion of these students are nontraditional and elusive. These ads may help to establish the brand of a university and help them to gain name recognition. However, they have a noticeably short shelf life and minimal impact on student enrollment and revenue generation.*

On the other hand, marketing through personal brand and global contributions of credible scholars teaching in a program is low cost, high impact, and has a long shelf life. Until the arrival of for-profit universities that use high pressure sales tactics and TV ads on a national or global scale, credible academic programs attracted students by using university brand, alumni networks, and faculty reputation. Most universities turn down far more students than they accept; they use low acceptance rates as a badge of honor.

However, in a field as new as cybersecurity, faculty members with global name recognition in the field were non-existent when I joined the faculty ranks. Few had a doctoral degree in the field and even fewer had work experiences in the field. Most teaching faculty coming in from a wide range of fields, were not consistent in spelling, defining, or explaining cybersecurity; computer scientists thought it is simply the security aspects of their discipline.

Therefore, I focused my efforts to educate as many people as possible, as quickly as possible, through articles, books, social media, public speaking, and countless one on one conversations. I made myself accessible to people at conferences, networked with everyone, and patiently responded to their questions about the field and about academic programs in the field.

During these engagements, I consciously performed several key personal branding and marketing activities.

BUILDING MY BRAND THROUGH KNOWLEDGE SHARING

DR. MANSUR HASIB, CISSP, PMP, CPHIMS
Global Award Winning Education and Business Leader,
Keynote Speaker, and Author
Education - Leadership - Marketing - Branding - Communications - Public Speaking

Winner www.cybersecurityleadership.com
https://www.linkedin.com/in/mansurhasib/   Twitter: @mhasib

Website/Business Card: Reflects Personal Brand
Daily Newspaper: Cybersecurity Leader
Books, Writings, Presentations
Content Marketing
People Networks
Helping People Succeed Reflects Back
www.cybersecurityleadership.com

Building My Brand Through Knowledge Sharing

8.5.2 Website and Business Card

I developed a rich website surrounding my passion for Cybersecurity Leadership: https://www.cybersecurityleadership.com/. I ensured that some content on my website would change daily so people would have a reason to come back. I also provided rich educational videos pulled down from my YouTube channel. Anytime I entered a contest, I provided easy voting buttons on my website.

Due to the rich content and constant updates, people return to the website and refer others to it. The website contains links to my speaking events, reviews, a daily newspaper, and links to my sales portal. People can also order signed and personalized books and #DrCybersecurity T-shirts from my website.

I also provide cross-links to other websites where my work or news about me has been published. These Search Engine Optimization techniques help my website rise in the search rankings - all at zero marketing expenses.

The Giant Crested Saguaro as the symbol of my personal brand consistently appears in my presentation slides, business cards, name tags, and all promotional materials. Many people spurn business cards with the idea that in this digital world, business cards are no longer needed. Wrong!

If fewer people are doing something, that alone might make you stand out. If they ask you why you are still giving out business cards when you could possibly scan a QR Code, that alone will spark a rich conversation. Your business card reflects your personal brand. Handing it out might be the primary ice breaking gesture that generates questions and a conversation.

Well thought out business cards will generate questions. *Questions create conversations. Conversations create relationships. Relationships create trust. Trust creates business!*

8.5.3 Making the Most of Networking

Networking is my most favorite activity at any event. I enjoy the company of people. Going up to anyone, smiling, and saying hello has always been natural to me. This is also a practiced skill. You will need to develop your own style of networking to make the most of these opportunities to meet people. Practice this art and you will excel at it.

Always remember that the primary goal of networking is building relationships. Think of this as farming. If you till the soil well, plant enough seeds, take care of them, you will enjoy bumper crops for years to come. A robust network will unlock amazing unadvertised opportunities for you! Some of the best jobs are never advertised!

Do not ask questions such as: Are you hiring? Do you have jobs? Can you help me get a job? Such questions may destroy your chance to build a relationship. You need to get to know the person first. You need to build a relationship. If you come across as a taker, you will turn off people.

At any conference you should not only network with speakers and attendees but also the vendors and sponsors who have set up display booths. Do not worry about being spammed. You can always use junk mail controls or call blocking to manage any spam you may get. Sponsors with booths need traffic and they will welcome your visit. Many booths will have the company CEO or a senior executive present.

Ask them about their company culture. What do they like? Do people support and help each other? How did they transition into the company? How did their career grow in the company? Have they had layoffs? If so, how frequently do they have layoffs? Strive to make a relationship with the person - not the company! If you can connect at the human level with someone, that person might lobby for hiring you into the company.

If you are a student or a job seeker, it is vital for you to network with all vendors. Once again, having a business card to give out as the opening gambit will make the conversation easier. Ask vendors about their company and products. If you are looking for a job, ask them if you can visit their company to learn more about their company.

Always let them ask you if you are looking for a job or in the market. Let them tell you about positions they may be looking to fill. Instead of directly telling them you are seeking a job, tell them you are trying to learn as much as possible about as many companies as possible and would like to visit several companies to learn about them.

Everything in this world revolves around people. Your success will depend on people. The more people in your network, the more will be your opportunities for success. Be passionate about building relationships with people and you will be amazed. You will develop the magic touch!

Here are some things that worked for my style:

1. Warm open smile and genuine openness to meeting people and getting to know them. Instead of focusing on myself, I focus on getting to know them. People always enjoy when you are genuinely interested in them.

2. I ask them an appropriate question for the setting. My favorite question is, "What is your passion?" This question is such a powerful icebreaker that others have started to use it. Other favorites are, "What is your favorite childhood memory?" "What are some things you find inspiring? These questions are neutral, and anyone can answer them appropriately. I recommend avoiding the following types of questions: What do you do? Who do you work for? How many children do you have? Are you married? How would someone unemployed respond to this? What about someone who works at home as a parent? We need to ask questions everyone will be comfortable answering.

3. At some point I give them my business card and say, "Here is my business card; I am happy to take yours if you have one." Once again, this gesture could lead to multiple questions and conversations. If I get a card from someone, I write notes on the back about anything I need to follow up with. Sometimes, I write down important points about the person or the conversation.

4. Afterwards, I follow up with a connection request. Perhaps I might send an introductory email providing links to helpful content. Sometimes, I address the issues I wrote down in my notes on the back of their cards.

During a networking event hosted by a vendor at their offices, I walked up to someone, handed him my card, and asked, "What is your passion?" The gentleman was extremely impressed and surprised by that question. He then excitedly told me how he had retired from the armed services and was now helping other transitioning military people into civilian life.

We had one of the richest first conversations I can recall. We talked about my business card too. We then introduced each other to several people and really got to know each other. As we shook hands to say goodbye, I felt him slipping something into my palm. I looked at my palm and saw the coin. He had just coined me! This is an incredibly special gesture that members of the US Armed Services use to reward or thank someone!

8.5.4 Daily Newspaper: The Cybersecurity Leader

To get daily fresh content on my website, I linked my website to several RSS feeds with related content. These feeds are free and if we use reliable sites, we are likely to provide a great portal for useful media stories from around the world in a topic area of our choice. Using free tools, I also created a curated newspaper of my own titled The Cybersecurity Leader at https://paper.li/e-1449156910.

In the early days of this free newspaper tool, the free version was feature rich and I curated stories from roughly ten global sources to produce a rich useful newspaper for free. Recently, the free version has been stripped down to bare bones. So, I do not use or promote this as much anymore. However, while it lasted, this paper did help me produce great content daily.

8.5.5 Books, Writings, and Conferences

I developed freelance writing relationships - both unpaid and paid for a wide range of online and in print magazines. Initially, it was hard to get paid assignments. However, within a couple of years, I was able to get paid writing assignments. Once this happened, I changed the relationship with other outlets.

If an organization wanted a free article, I asked them to write it themselves as an interview. An interview is far more powerful for brand promotional purposes. It reduces my work and allows less of my intellectual property to go out without compensation. Interviews with well-known newspapers or even local newspapers are all excellent for personal brand promotion.

Over the years, hundreds of such pieces are floating around on the internet. The following are a few examples (including one that a magazine editor wrote to get me more votes for a contest):

1. https://www.mic.com/articles/151215/a-future-with-neural-implants-means-hackers-can-remote-control-your-brain

2. http://www.bizmonthly.com/cami-presents-inaugural-cybersecurity-award-winners/

3. https://sensorstechforum.com/dr-mansur-hasib-cybersecurity-people-powered-perpetual-innovation/

4. https://infogovworld.com/ig-topics/an-interview-with-dr-mansur-hasib-cybersecurity-leader/

5. https://www.cyberthoughts.org/2018/12/the-cybersecurity-skills-shortage.html

6. https://healthmanagement.org/c/it/news/healthmanagement-org-contributor-nominated-for-cybersecurity-award

7. https://healthmanagement.org/c/it/post/zoom-on-dr-mansur-hasib-programme-chair-cybersecurity-technology-umuc-author-1

8. https://cyberstartupobservatory.com/cyber-startup-observatory-dr-mansur-hasib-cybersecurity-leader-of-the-week/

9. https://www.capitalgazette.com/business/cg-in-new-book-gambrills-resident-suggests-creating-a-culture-of-cybersecurity-20140801-story.html

10. https://www.grmdocumentmanagement.com/arma-info-con-2019-key-takeaways-from-the-conference/

Every time I won an award or published a book, opportunities for interviews and media stories increased. When I was asked to speak for free at conferences, I always negotiated something that would help me to promote my work and personal brand such as the following free display booth at CyberMaryland 2015. At this event, I announced my new com-

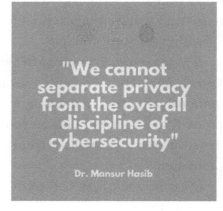

"We cannot separate privacy from the overall discipline of cybersecurity"

Dr. Mansur Hasib

Quote Graphic Prepared by Q1 Productions

petency based Master of Science and Doctor of Science programs in Cybersecurity that I had authored and shared the slides and descriptions of the programs as widely as possible. At the same event, I was also able to get free tickets for several graduate students who were thrilled to learn and network.

Cybersecurity Leadership booth at CyberMaryland 2015

8.5.6 Content Marketing

I noted that many of my quotes started to appear in Google images, articles, as well as various quotation sites! This was a stunning phenomenon. It meant that all those years of living and working certain values and sharing them with others using well developed speechcraft skills were finally paying off in a big way!

As these types of pieces appeared, I shared them with my professional network as regular content marketing posts. Constant posting of pure ads or self-promotional pieces can hurt a personal brand. However, if done as an informational piece and the article or message being posted is a useful educational piece, sharing will enhance a personal brand.

Similarly, one to two minutes or even longer educational videos will also help promote a personal brand. Ideally, these should not contain a call to purchase services or a book - that is a definite put off - even though many traditional marketing advisors would suggest it. I do not find these calls to be useful. Instead, I get better results and more personal affiliation from my network by using pure content pieces. There are multiple other ways to find our books or services to purchase.

Many of my videos were produced by conference organizers who had invited me to speak. Many speakers are not comfortable producing videos on short notice. They may need multiple takes before an acceptable video can be produced.

However, as a professional speaker with years of Toastmasters training, I can sit down and chat with anyone at length on a wide range of topics and produce a high quality video in a single take! This skill made it easy for organizers. Once at a recent conference, I was given six minutes of studio time and I produced a two minute video in roughly four minutes!

I needed a second take because they had not informed me I needed to keep my feet planted. I am used to moving around, and I moved closer to the camera to share an important message thinking they would actively follow the speaker! Well, they did not, and this movement had taken me out of the camera frame!

Polishing public speaking skills and always being available to do an interview on short notice are specially important. This is also why at any organization I worked in, I was a sought after spokesperson about the organization, its mission, teaching models, and accomplishments. This is also why these organizations felt comfortable letting me talk with media or international visitors at any time.

8.5.7 Showing Up

More than half of life's success happens to people who show up. Show up and magic will happen. We can never get the job we never applied for. The number of free networking opportunities available at any given day or month is simply amazing. Simply showing up will lead to chance meetings, connections, conversations, and opportunities. An incredible proportion of opportunities are never advertised!

If we sit at home and bide away our time watching TV or doing some passive activity or simply waiting for an opportunity to come our way, it will never happen. Life takes living. Living requires being with people. People do business with people. A chance meeting could change everything!

ARMA InfoCon 2019 Opening Keynote, Nashville, TN

In 2014, I was working on a state of Maryland project as a contractor. I was being paid by the hour, but I was not allowed to work beyond forty hours. I had no reason to work on weekends. If I did, I would not get paid for it because the contracting company I was working through, would not authorize any overtime.

However, I have always led my life doing the right thing in any job. I knew the work I was doing was meaningful and critical. The initial roll out of the system had been disastrous and people were having serious technical problems. Once a person encountered a problem, their health insurance was stuck - they could not get through the system to obtain health insurance through the state marketplace.

I had figured out ways to solve a vast majority of problems. Every individual problem I solved meant someone just got healthcare! That was huge to me. Even though I had written solution guides and trained hundreds of agents to solve these problems, my technical support presence was always appreciated by all workers.

So, I volunteered to show up for various weekend health fairs around the state where the Maryland Health Benefit Exchange had invited members of the public to come and sign up for health insurance. People with problems were specially encouraged to come in person with their documentation so we could solve their problems.

With **Representative Elijah Cummings** at Health Insurance Fair, 2014

At one of these health fairs, I happened to show up on the same day several Maryland dignitaries also decided to show up. I got to meet Governor Martin O'Malley, Senator Ben Cardin, and Representative Elijah Cummings - all on the same day! Since I am always prepared for these types of occasions, I took the opportunities to walk up to them, introduce myself, and request a photo. They all graciously obliged and I made some priceless memories.

With **Governor Martin O'Malley** at Health Insurance Fair, 2014

Governor Martin O'Malley was extremely gracious. He thanked me for volunteering and for the work we were doing in helping to get people insurance and even put his hand around me as he posed for this picture! Note that a copy of my book Cybersecurity Leadership is on the ledge behind the Governor's chair!

Later when I participated in the Maryland Association of Counties (MACo) Conference in 2019 to showcase our leadership in cybersecurity academic programs and to explain the field to leaders from Maryland agencies and companies, I saw Senator Ben Cardin again and once again he obliged with a photograph.

With Maryland Senator Ben Cardin at MACo 2019 Conference

When I took this picture with Senator Ben Cardin, I was able to mention the earlier meeting back in 2014. While he might not remember that he met me, everyone in the Maryland government knew about the technical issues with enrollment related to the health insurance exchanges during that time. Recognizing possible common threads to bring up, will always create opportunities for conversations. That is the key. If you can generate conversations, you can create relationships!

Showing up matters a lot! Doing things that no one else will do, matters greatly. I was not making any extra money. This was not part of my job responsibilities. As a matter of fact, the entire effort ate into my personal time. However, as a leader, I know the value of my participation and what it means in terms of making connections and recruiting students.

Academic executives with no practical experiences outside of academia are unlikely to understand the value of the effort, because their frame of thinking is different; they are unlikely to have noted the tectonic shift happening in marketing or student recruitment.

Strangely enough, at many academic institutions, speaking and attending conferences are viewed as a perk or a boondoggle. Although I have seen academic executives abuse their positions by travelling to events at exotic foreign countries using university funds, scholarly faculty and student participation at large professional conferences usually result in enhanced reputation for the programs and result in additional students. For me, this has been the cheapest way to attract lots of students. When I am an invited speaker, my expenses are typically covered by the organizers.

However, most university executives without outside experience do not understand the modern world of marketing. They expect student recruitment to be the Marketing and Enrollment department's job, and do not realize the world of marketing has changed. Most of these departments do not leverage technology; instead, they use expensive travel and visits with severe geographic limitations. In today's world we need to rethink many older models that used to work in the past.

We are the only people who know what we can and cannot do; we should never let others define our limitations. The wider our range of abilities, the stronger will be our inherent source of power and ability to produce value. If we assume someone else will be doing something, it may never get done!

If we recognize something must be done, and we know we can do it without impacting our primary responsibilities, we must step up to do it. In most cases, specially in the private sector, companies will appreciate the initiative and innovation. That is what leadership and value production is all about. These are all opportunities to build personal brands, continue to refine our greatness, and serve our clients and customers well!

At the MACo event, more surprises awaited us. First, Maryland's First Lady Yumi Hogan suddenly arrived with her photographer and took pictures with us in our booth and later posted them on their website for us to download. This was a wonderful gesture, and we were all talking about it. Then suddenly, Gover-

With Maryland Governor Larry Hogan at MACo 2019

nor Larry Hogan himself came around with his own coterie and chatted with us.

He browsed through the awards and quipped about them. The awards became conversation pieces! We were the only booth with awards. Since we had so many of them, some people joked if we were selling them - once again these engagements became opportunities for memorable conversations. These conversations led to student leads. Student leads led to enrollment.

If I had a plain standard display with mostly marketing materials and swags, we would have truly little to talk about. The students also gained simply because they showed up. They did not have to take the trouble to come; many students who were offered the same chance did not come. However, by coming and volunteering to help me, the students made valuable connections with people they would never have met and created unforgettable memories. That is the power of showing up!

With Anchor Elsa M. at Midday Maryland, WMAR-TV, ABC Channel 2

My willingness to show up and speak to any audience on short notice, led to many unexpected adventures, connections, and presentation opportunities with international delegations, several Governor's meetings, several international keynote opportunities, and even an appearance on WMAR Channel 2 Baltimore where I recorded an episode in a single take.

Opening Keynote at the 2019 International Medical Education Leaders Forum, Kuwait

When I made the opening keynote presentation in front of a Chilean delegation, I was asked the night before because the scheduled university executive had fallen ill. I once moderated a Chief Information Security Officer (CISO) panel of three Fortune 500 CISOs with similar notice. I made a self-deprecating opening remark about being an understudy and not the real star of the show. I explained how my wife thinks understudies are critical for the success of any effort; and how I had made a career out of being an understudy. Everyone laughed and we all had a great session.

People who are ready to show up and can deliver results on short notice, always get more opportunities for success; each success leads to more successes. *Always be ready. Do not wait for the opportunity to arrive first.* Many reliable studies show that people with strong public speaking skills can increase their lifetime earnings by 50% or more. That is a remarkable way to give yourself a pay raise!

In 2019 when I appeared in a TV interview on ABCs WMAR Channel 2 Baltimore, I was able to display both my book and award. This happened simply because I thought to bring them along! No one asked me to. I did not ask anyone either. Similarly, another time I showed up for a Facebook Live interview with the (ISC)[2] award guitar in hand! Every marketing opportunity must be milked for maximum benefit! *Give people a reason to remember you.*

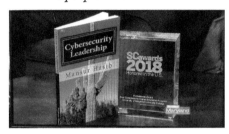

WMAR-TV, ABC Channel 2, May 2019

People always prefer proven and reliable people. This is also true about media interviews. No one expects perfection when we show up on short notice. So, when we surprise them with a high quality product, they become our fans forever.

I remember multiple situations where our university needed a speaker at a conference. However, no one was willing to volunteer. They could not quickly tailor an existing presentation for a different audience; most did not have a collection of ready to go presentations. For me, such adaptation took little time or effort.

When asked, I agreed and delivered every time. With hundreds of presentations in my repertoire, I am always ready to present on almost any topic with little or no notice. This flexibility allowed me to present at many interdisciplinary conferences, which also resulted in my work being exposed to a wider audience. Such range can be developed simply through study, practice, and development of the brain in a variety of disciplines and issues we may have an interest in.

Sometimes, the key is to figure out the right way to connect to the audience. Making the connection to the audience is critical. We cannot take the same presentation and expect it to work at different venues without modification.

For example, at several Women's Leadership conferences when I spoke, I shared stories of how I learned leadership from my mother from an early age and how these lessons helped me to become successful.

Strangely enough, I found that mothers are typically not viewed as leaders - even though most children gain their early life lessons from their mothers!

Another time, I was invited to deliver an afternoon keynote about Cybersecurity Leadership at Elevate Women in front of several hundred women executives and elected officials in Canada. I sat through the whole morning listening to others to prepare my opening remarks, which would tie my talk to the audience. Opening remarks are critical for connecting with the audience; learning about the audience and framing the remarks within the context of the previous speakers will help.

After listening to several speakers, I assessed the dominant problem appeared to be entrenched male power and the struggle to wage an asymmetric and uphill battle against this power. I decided to suggest a fresh message. I urged them to stop playing someone else's game that is already rigged against them. I suggested that they change the game and develop a new source of power by embracing Cybersecurity Leadership and they would soon dominate the new field.

This method of tying the message to the problems identified at the event, always resonates with any audience. I did the same thing before another major keynote on Cybersecurity Leadership in front of records managers and information governance professionals at ARMA 2019. I went a day early and networked with as many attendees as possible and tailored the opening so it would appeal to the entire audience.

Showing up with a mentor or at the invitation of a mentor or someone with a strong personal brand can make the effort even more productive. A mentor can make targeted introductions with influential people and leaders in a field. Such introductions act as endorsements and immediately impart a higher level of credibility to anyone.

If a mentor asks you to attend something, make every effort to attend. In any major conference where thousands of people are in attendance, it is exceedingly difficult for someone new to a field to meet the right people. However, an established leader in the field can give you more confidence and ease the process.

I almost always negotiate free attendance for my students to events I participate in. Once I was able to take fifty students to a major conference. I took thirty to another event, and twenty five to another. I know magic happened to all who showed up! Some even got hired on the spot! Some got hired later. Such is the power of showing up!

8.5.7.1 A Student Example of the Power of Showing Up

#MathWhiz Elena Healing started her graduate cybersecurity studies in my Cybersecurity Leadership and Governance class. During my classes, I explained cybersecurity and the importance of leadership. I also explained that leadership is a practiced art form. Everyone already has this skill in them; they just need to develop and master it.

Elena was intrigued. She had already established a great career in Mathematics and Statistics but did not realize she could rise to greater heights. She listened intently and when I invited the entire class to a free conference where I would be exhibiting my books, she showed up.

In fact, she was the only student from all my classes who showed up! At the event, she bought a signed copy of my book Cybersecurity Leadership. This book and my class about Cybersecurity Leadership and Governance intrigued her so much that she decided to research the topic further; she understood how she could merge leadership into her professional life to propel her career upward.

Elena Healing graduated in 2019, obtained a new supervisory role and has been carving a new path upward for her career. During her job interview, when asked to discuss her supervisory experiences, she honestly stated that she had no job experience as a supervisor, but she had researched the topic of leadership and team building deeply and read various books. She then shared her understanding of leadership learned from her mentor and explained how she would be able to form teams and bring out their best talents because she had internalized these principles from my book.

Elena Healing Graduating with a Master of Science, 2019

If she had not chosen to show up at the conference, or take an interest in my classes or book, the new trajectory of her career might never have materialized. Her initiative to show up helped her discover leadership skills that she never knew she had! She shared her story of merging leadership with mathematics during two powerful presentations with the Cybersecurity Divas.

8.5.8 People Networks

My efforts started to help so many people all over the world that I soon gained a global following with regular invitations to speak at major events or be interviewed by some magazine, newspaper, or podcaster.

In 2018, I was inducted into the Hall of Fame by the Global Cybersecurity Observatory based in Spain. They produced the following badge for me to use on my slides and business cards.

Cybersecurity Observatory, Spain

In 2018 and 2019 the Master of Science in Cybersecurity Technology program I designed, launched, and grew from 1,500 students to serve almost 5,000 students globally, won back to back awards from SC Magazine as the Best Cybersecurity Higher Education Program in the USA.

 This was an unprecedented

In addition, several earned media pieces with my ideas and quotations were published both online and in print. These pieces benefited me and the organization I was affiliated with for several months.

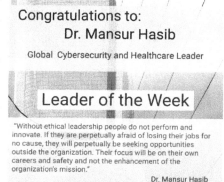

Congratulations to:
Dr. Mansur Hasib
Global Cybersecurity and Healthcare Leader

Leader of the Week

"Without ethical leadership people do not perform and innovate. If they are perpetually afraid of losing their jobs for no cause, they will perpetually be seeking opportunities outside the organization. Their focus will be on their own careers and safety and not the enhancement of the organization's mission."

Dr. Mansur Hasib

www.cyberstartupobservatory.com

achievement for the university **Winner** and the free earned media advertising and the resulting enrollment increases were astounding! As soon as I left, with no one else working to defend the crown, another university immediately won the award in 2020 and the sheen vanished! In addition, there was a dramatic decline in enrollment across all cybersecurity programs followed by more layoffs.

In July of 2019, at a ceremony held in Toronto, Canada, the ICSIC Conference, after reviewing more than 250 global nominations, awarded me the 2019 Outstanding Global Cybersecurity Leadership Award. Once again this resulted in increased attention, increased inquiries and increased enrollments. Throughout the promotion of the conference and well after the conclusion of the award ceremony, I enjoyed plenty of cross brand promotion and earned media marketing.

ICSIC 2019 Cybersecurity Conference Award winners, L-R: Dr. Mansur Hasib for Outstanding Global Cybersecurity Leadership; Lisa Reshaur (for Bret Arsenault) of Microsoft, for International Cybersecurity Leadership; Dr. Arash Habibi Lashkari of the University of New Brunswick, for Cybersecurity Education; Rima Aristocrat of Willis College, for Women in Cybersecurity; with Yomi Olalere host of ICSIC 2019

ICSIC 2019 @ICSIC_Canada · 21h

Don't miss Award Winning Cyber Security and Healthcare Leader, Author, Keynote Speaker, and Media Commentator @mhasib at this year's International #CyberSecurity and #Intelligence Conference in #Toronto July 16-18! icsicanada.org #icsic2019 #studentswelcome

Example of an earned media post by ICSIC 2019 Conference

Stories of these awards were submitted by the university administration to the Maryland Higher Education Commission as evidence of maintaining high standards of education as part of the Academic Program Review and accreditation renewal package submitted in 2019. These stories were also forwarded by the university administration to the University System of Maryland Chancellor's office as university accomplishments. The Chancellor's report to the Board of Regents contained these stories several times!

8.5.9 Helping People Succeed Reflects Back

I also helped several of my colleagues win awards by campaigning for them. I found that my passionate network was willing to vote for any candidate I endorsed. My personal brand had the power to reflect positively whenever I lent it to an organization or person. This was a fascinating discovery.

While I was with UMUC, I helped my supervisor Dr. Emma Garrison-Alexander win the 2018 People's Choice Award in Cybersecurity. The following year, I campaigned and helped Dr. Loyce Pailen win the 2019 People's Choice Award in Cybersecurity. Both efforts helped us increase enrollment and earned us free media attention.

All Cybersecurity Association of Maryland award winners are permanently listed here and they continue to give all of us personal brand promotion: https://www.mdcyber.com/md_cyber_awards_recipients.php. I also discovered that by helping others win, I was enhancing my own personal brand. There is tremendous power in such cross-brand promotion.

In general, I campaigned for any friend in my network. This usually meant that these same friends would help me when I competed in any contest. During and after the contests we could promote our brands every day - simply by soliciting votes or by sharing the standings! These types of social media based free brand promotions provide far better results than multi-million dollar TV ads!

In addition, when I took students and graduates to events, they also became powerful brand ambassadors. Other attendees heard their stories and observed their knowledge and professionalism and wanted to join the movement. These activities helped me recruit thousands of students -- all at zero cost to the institution!

8.6 OPPORTUNITIES IN ADVERSITY

While many people are frozen with inaction at a time of uncertainty or unplanned adversity, I always focus on actions within my control and look for ways to solve the problem, minimize its negative impact, help others in some manner, and continue to build my personal brand.

The global pandemic of 2020, which hit the USA most acutely, challenged me just as dramatically as it did everyone else. I was forced to move all my teaching, speaking, and networking activities to 100% online. I had to pay extra attention to the undergraduate students because most of them were not used to online classes; they were also shell-shocked with the disruption to their lives.

However, I went on overdrive once I observed that people need positive ways to engage with others and must keep their minds occupied. Many were losing jobs and internships. Many were losing family members and friends. The news on TV was depressing. Our Toastmasters club meetings and contests were all cancelled. I looked for positive solutions within my control.

I immediately moved our Toast of Severna Park Toastmasters club meetings online and began to offer training to anyone who needed it. I then hosted our Division's International Speech Contest online and trained all the contestants. I wrote instructions and passed them on to the District leadership. I started to promote our online club meetings on social media.

These activities resulted in many new friendships and connections with Toastmasters members globally. Our club gained several new members from outside the Maryland region, including an international member. I started a weekly podcast with global guests, initially thinking that I would only do this occasionally.

However, due to an unprecedented level of interest, so far I have talked with over eighty global guests and engaged in more than two hundred topics and questions! We even experimented with a humorous skit on ransomware for Cybersecurity Month 2020 and people laughed so much that they warned others not to watch it with a drink in their hand!

I allowed anyone in my network to join as featured guests to ask me questions on any personal development or cybersecurity topic for fifteen minutes in a recorded conversation. No one needed to be an expert in my shows. Thus, many students and new professionals in the field were able to make their debut on my show.

These conversations became extremely popular and my work spread even more widely globally. I set up free registration for all events on Eventbrite and placed videos, schedules, and registration information on a special page on my website:

https://www.cybersecurityleadership.com/conversations.html

To create a more professional looking show, I created Virtual Backgrounds specially for each type of activity I was doing online.

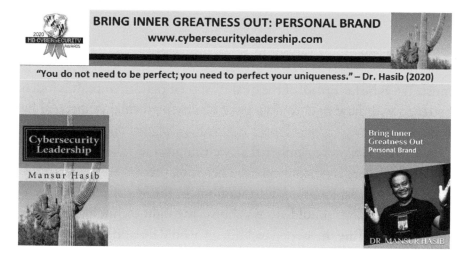

As I gained experience, we decided to expand and experiment some more. I organized and coached a team of my former graduate students to make high quality innovative and lively presentations and helped them apply to speak at several professional conferences. This initiative gave birth to the Cybersecurity Divas, who immediately gained a global following!

I also taught them to avoid exploitative situations, protect the quality of their presentations and to be careful about giving away intellectual property for free. The following recent example is worth sharing as a common situation to avoid.

We had been accepted to present for one hour at a respectable online conference. We were listed on the website and the conference received hundreds of registrations due to our marketing. Suddenly, one week before the presentation, we learned the first half of our time slot would be preceded by two other speakers doing an infomercial about their organization.

Even though we had agreed on a technology and prepared for it, we were given additional technical restrictions on what we could and could not do. We were assigned a Master of Ceremonies who would control our session! They even wanted copies of our slides and wanted us to sign a release giving them and their sponsors the right to use our presentations to market themselves without any compensation or credit to us.

The audacity was shocking to all of us. While such ridiculous and exploitative situations can occur every now and then, everyone needs to watch out for them. I have little tolerance for them. A performer must always be in control of the quality of their performance. It is much better to withdraw than to do a poor quality performance dictated by someone else!

We must always remember that we bring value to any conference. Without us there is no conference! Therefore, there is no reason to tolerate or enable exploitation. Furthermore, in the age of plentiful technology choices, we should always choose the right technology suitable for our goal. Using the wrong technology would be akin to using out of tune poor quality musical instruments provided by concert organizers instead of using our own.

The debut of our innovative show was about to be ruined in front of a global audience and no one would know why! A low quality presentation would be useless to all of us! *We only have one opportunity to make a first impression!* On top of that we had no desire to lose control of our intellectual property to allow others to make money or advertise their organizations using our work without paying us anything! So, we decided to withdraw our participation and host the show ourselves.

Within three weeks we hosted our own grand experiment - the Cybersecurity Divas Global Tour 2020 on July 31, 2020 at 8pm US EST. After a lot of research, we chose this time because it would be a reasonable time of day for many parts of the world. We genuinely wanted a global audience.

Eventually, we received registrations from twenty nine countries globally and seven of us made short innovative presentations; all providing valuable information within seven minutes or less each! Our goal was to teach everyone globally that conference presentations do not have to be boring hour-long monologues by a single speaker reading from slides. We also wanted to change the boring and disorganized nature of typical panels where the moderator or a single panel member filibusters for a large portion of the time. The entire forty two minute event turned out to be an action packed mini-conference!

We made sure all slides were colorful and exciting with large readable fonts. We all helped each other with our presentations and provided constructive feedback during every practice session. The final execution was like a well-rehearsed harmony of virtuosos. As moderator I did not wish to waste time by having each speaker revert back to me. So, we practiced transitioning smoothly from one speaker to the next. This type of transition gave the audience a smooth experience. In an online format smooth transitions are incredibly important!

The Cybersecurity Divas Global Tour 2020 opened with a Tomiko Evans CyberRap titled *Cybersecurity Divas* as we showed slides with the bios of each speaker for roughly two minutes. This innovation even made the introductions an entertaining feature. I then made some introductory remarks and provided a short explanation of the cybersecurity model.

Then, Katoria Henry made a sports themed presentation on cybersecurity in the style of a sportscaster. This was followed by Katia Dean injecting her humor into a presentation using comics to describe transitioning into cybersecurity and her job hunting experiences. Elena Healing shared her passion combining mathematics and leadership. Anye Biamby presented on cybersecurity policy using animation. Naalphatu Toure discussed international cybersecurity in the African region using gamification.

Finally, Tomiko Evans provided the grand finale with a medley of spoken words, CyberRap, music, and dance. The result was an unprecedented and historic presentation captured in the following video.

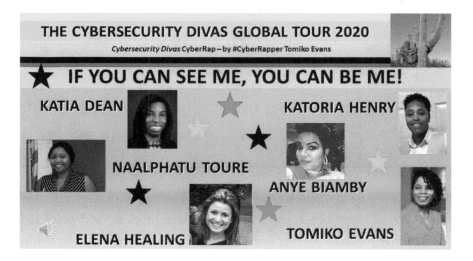

https://youtu.be/3C5u59Rw7Mw

During the most enjoyable networking session after the event and during future episodes of my podcasts, I was deeply touched to learn that people had tears in their eyes as they watched the innovative and creative performances. The special ingredient in this presentation was every Cybersecurity Diva's embrace of themselves.

No one tried to be like someone else. They each embraced their inner greatness and dared to express it in front of a global audience! Every presentation represented a new and unique way to make conference presentations. In addition, they explained an aspect of the cybersecurity model in a fun and engaging way so anyone from any field would understand the presentation.

Promoting events are excellent marketing and brand promotion activities. In addition, creating video recordings and posting these recordings on social media can continue brand promotion for a long time -- all at zero cost. If sponsors can be obtained for any of the shows, they can also produce income. With sufficient subscribers on YouTube or other platforms, people who produce videos can also make money selling ads.

8.7 GLOBAL NETWORKING

In the modern era, our success is critically dependent on our network. Other people with strong global brands can dramatically amplify our impact. Therefore, it is critical to build symbiotic relationships with others through business social media such as LinkedIn.

Many people make the mistake of thinking LinkedIn is simply an electronic resume. This is not true. People must complete their profiles with personally branded content, have professional pictures, recommendations, links to articles and videos, and a list of key accomplishments showing the value they represent to any hiring organization.

LinkedIn can be a global representation of our Personal Brand! Just as the results (or lack thereof) of a Google search can hurt a job seeker, an incomplete profile on LinkedIn can also damage the personal brand value of a candidate. Our people network will determine our net worth; they will create opportunities we would never receive otherwise. Sometimes, they will help us find amazing jobs without making any applications. Some of the best jobs are never advertised!

During the pandemic, my friend Rima Aristocrat, current Chair and former President and CEO of the historic Willis College of Canada was invited by Dr. Bryce Fabro to speak on Cybersecurity Leadership and education at the HERO Brainshare 2020 online conference being hosted out of Singapore. She insisted that the organizers invite me as well to join her in her presentation. What resulted was another amazing event.

The organizers prepared amazing video introductions and special Virtual Backgrounds for us. They collected snippets of our work, previous presentations, thoughts, and ideas to prepare mind blowing video introductions, which were not only used to promote the event but also served as our introductions during the event. This was not a boring introduction by someone reading from a script. It was a symphony: https://youtu.be/Gwb61n3EeWI

The final presentation on June 26th, 2020 8pm US EST, which was June 27th in Singapore, Philippines and India, a global audience watched this amazing event for roughly two hours. The most fascinating thing about these brand building activities is that everyone associated with the activity benefits. Even the people who share and comment on the videos and posts, benefit. With each activity, our global professional network continues to expand. Since I make the effort to respond to all comments to the extent possible, this engagement creates an even stronger personal brand affinity with others!

The best part - everything happens at no cost. There is no need for fancy expensive advertising, which has a noticeably short shelf life. Instead, the educational content with a long shelf life continues to market everyone for many years because it continues to be shared and viewed. In addition, an old post can be revived every now and then for the benefit of new connections. This is the future of marketing!

Online HERO Brainshare Global Conference 2020, Singapore

https://youtu.be/JlRLXJ-OeQI

8.8 CROSS BRAND PROMOTION

Cross brand promotion is one of the best ways to get free high value brand promotion in social media. I was surprised by how few traditional marketers understand this; they do not want to provide links or mention other companies on their websites. They are constantly seeking fifteen or thirty minute meetings trying to sell their products.

No one has the time to talk to thousands of connections one on one unless they are getting a benefit or getting paid for their time! I view these conversations as consultations - any time I spend learning about someone's product is nothing more than a consultation to me. Instead, they may have better luck with cross brand promotional relationships; cross brand promotion is just as powerful as earned media!

When my website contains a link to another website with a higher ranking, my website rises in the ranking. My decision to provide links on my website to my articles, news stories, interviews, or quotes on other websites, helped me dramatically. In addition, I also promote organizations that use and promote my work and they continue to do the same.

Sponsors of my work continue to receive marketing promotion several years after the event.

Cybersecurity Leadership Day at Willis College, Ottawa, Canada 2018

When I visited the historic Willis College in Ottawa, Canada, to deliver a keynote, I noted a big sign greeting everyone. Prior to the event, Willis College and other hosts of the event marketed the event heavily for several weeks. Both Willis College and I were able to use the opportunity to do cross brand promotion for mutual benefit. Such cross brand promotional activities can include pictures, stories, videos, and links. The cross brand promotion can continue for months or years. The stronger your network, the more opportunities for cross brand promotion.

Visiting with Rima Aristocrat, President and CEO of Willis College

8.8.1 Cross Brand Promotion through Influencers

All social media platforms have influencers who have already built strong personal brands themselves. Influencers understand the power of other influencers. We need influencers in the field we want to learn about. For example, if you want to learn about social media, you must learn from a social media influencer and strategist.

Think of influencers as media outlets in the traditional world. If you can get an influencer to feature you, mention your work, Share your work, Like your work, comment on your work, your personal brand gets free promotion like being mentioned by a major news outlet.

Influencers have credibility and a following and are essentially stars in their fields. They have achieved this stardom through the development, promotion, and projection of their personal brands. Anyone, of any age can be an influencer today. So, keep your minds open about the influencers you choose to follow and engage with.

In 2018, I was still trying to understand social media and the use of hashtags. Since I have always been liberal about making connections with people of a wide range of fields, I was already connected with Marisa Cali, Founder of All the Social.

After following Marisa Cali's posts and engaging with them, I realized she has a strong understanding of social media. So, I continued to follow. At that time, she was experimenting with the tagline CEO of Hashtags. I thought it was bold and innovative. I could tell she knew her inner greatness and was not afraid to bring it out; she was also unafraid of experimenting.

I saw her experiments and I found them intriguing! One day, I saw a post from her offering to help people in her network with hashtag suggestions. After a few message exchanges, she declared I should use #Dr-Cybersecurity to organize my most important posts.

"Your brand clearly projects this," she said. "Wouldn't it be hokey or presumptuous?" I asked. "Don't do it all the time. Experiment and use it for the most important posts and see how people respond. You can use multiple hashtags," she said. I followed her advice.

Suddenly #DrCybersecurity became my most well-known nick-name! I saw other people sharing my work and posts with this hashtag. We all noted that this hashtag and brand had become synonymous with me. Even when other people posted to this hashtag, it ended up promoting my brand because of the dominance of my personal brand and the sheer number of posts I had already contributed to that hashtag.

During DC Startup Week 2019, I decided to support another influencer friend in the field of communications and attended her speaking session. I was sitting in the front row and could not see people behind me. Suddenly a young woman came up to me and shocked me with the question, "Aren't you Dr. Cybersecurity?"

With Marisa Cali, Founder of All the Social at DC Startup Week, 2019

It was Marisa Cali. I recognized her right away even though we had never met in person before. It was fascinating. We had influenced each other's work profoundly for a couple of years without ever meeting in person or even talking on the phone! She was there to support two of her friends who were speaking, and we met purely by accident.

One evening I met several friends of Tomiko Evans while having a late dinner at a random restaurant inside Universal Studios in Florida with a childhood friend! Tomiko and her friends were seated at the table right next to us! To top it all, Tomiko was wearing a #DrCybersecurity T-shirt! I once told Tomiko, "Just show up and magic will happen."

With Noureen Njoroge and Tomiko Evans, Florida, 2019

If we put ourselves out there, these wonderful accidents will become quite common. It is all about relationships - genuine relationships and continuous learning from each other. Relationships will lead to cross sales - however sales should never be the ulterior motive, or you will fail to build relationships! Take time to build relationships with influencers and you will be amazed at the results.

Always remember that a relationship is a two way street. If you are solely engaged in self-promotion or the promotion of your own company, you will not make it as an influencer. Influencers always give value to their network. You must engage and support each other's posts, and both will enjoy cross influencer promotion - all at no cost!

In general, it is not a good idea to try to sell to a cross-brand promoting partner. That could damage the relationship. Even if you feel one of your paid services could help, let the other party seek out your paid services. In general, cross brand promoters and influencers are worth their value simply for appearing with you. Would you rather have a onetime payment and lose the long-term cross brand promotion relationship?

The primary value of cross brand promotion partners is promoting your overall business and you theirs. Such promotion must be bilateral! In social media, one way relationships do not last. I have no reason to engage or promote services or posts from people who are never engaging or promoting my posts. Relationships are fragile and must be nurtured.

8.9 NEVER RESTING ON LAURELS

Personal branding is still marketing - but of a dramatically different kind. Like marketing, there must be constant messaging and content that promotes the personal brand. However, the most powerful way to promote a personal brand is to win awards.

We should not try to win the same award several years in a row. In most cases, the same person is not even allowed to compete two years in a row. However, after a short two to three year respite while helping others win, it is perfectly okay to try to win an award for the second time.

The best part is that all finalists get to compete in the People's Choice Award which is decided by global public voting. This has always been my strength!

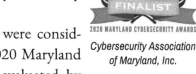

Cybersecurity Association of Maryland, Inc.

In total, eighty four nominations were considered across seven categories for the 2020 Maryland Cybersecurity Awards. Entries were evaluated by twelve independent judges whose roles ranged from Vice Presidents to Founders.

In August, the association announced I had made it into the final three in the Champion of the Year category. Thus, along with all twenty one finalists in seven categories, I became eligible to compete in the 2020

People's Choice Award in Cybersecurity. I campaigned in earnest once again.

Organizers gave us plenty of marketing materials such as the following to help campaign and promote our personal brands. Even if we never win, these campaigns are free opportunities for brand promotion, and everyone must take advantage of them. However, strangely enough, most people never realize this and never campaign even when they are finalists.

This time, I was in a far stronger position than in 2017. My global network was now quadruple what it was back then. My work has become far more established during the last three years. I also have the experience of knowing how to campaign and pace the solicitations for votes. It was also noticeably clear from the very outset that my community of supporters would be passionately campaigning for me.

The posts and independent unsolicited campaigning by others were very heartwarming. This is what everyone must strive to achieve - the genuine love and support of a community. That is when you know you are touching and helping people and they are benefiting from your work and knowledge.

That is the essence of greatness. If your personal brand activities are not benefiting countless others, you cannot be great. People must be impacted positively by your contributions. As my older brother once told me more than thirty years ago, "Live your life in such a way that strangers will mourn your death." This powerful statement has inspired me ever since!

8.10 EARNED MEDIA

Winning in any contest means several stories and press releases in a wide range of forums. Sometimes, members of the press will interview us and write feature stories. Even the announcement of a win in front of thousands of people during an awards ceremony earns us valuable free publicity for our personal brands and the organizations we may be representing at that time. The networking before and after the awards event is priceless!

In most cases our names and organizational names may be immortalized on the websites of the organizers and continue to give us brand promotion for years after the event. In addition, it will usually lead to print and video interviews at a global scale. Earned media is the best way to receive powerful brand promotion at no cost. It is also the most credible.

Being prepared to win is also key. For example, if there is a chance that you will be asked to make an acceptance speech, make sure you have a memorable speech ready. The video and story of your win must be powerful and memorable. If it is not, you will miss making the most of the opportunity! A video lasts a long time! Make the most of *every* opportunity.

As soon as the finalists for the 2020 Maryland Cybersecurity Awards were announced, organizers asked us to send them pictures, bios, and a short video expressing our excitement, which would be played if we won the award. Given that this was a virtual event, I knew boring videos or plain formal headshots would not entertain people. Such artifacts for a virtual event must be completely rethought!

So, after three days of thinking and several experiments and feedback from trusted people in my network, I provided two videos. One video had been produced by a conference in Singapore as my introduction for that event. In the other, I put two keyboards together using MIDI, slung the acoustic electric guitar on my shoulders, put up my conference banner, and produced a music video singing a bar from an old song I grew up with that I thought would be appropriate for the occasion.

Note that I decided to bring all of myself to the effort! If I can do things others cannot, why not do them! I knew no one else would do this. However, if I did win and my videos were played, they would make an instant impact that would last a long time! Videos have a long shelf life.

My efforts paid off in a big way on September 16, 2020, when, during a virtual event, I won both the 2020 Cybersecurity Champion of the

Year and the 2020 People's Choice Award in Cybersecurity in the 2020 Maryland Cybersecurity Awards!

The organizers gave me the following badges to be used in my email signatures, websites, and various marketing materials.

 In addition, I received two trophies for the 2020 awards. All artifacts are now integral to my personal branding and market-  ing efforts anytime I have a book signing event, table display, or booth at any conference, festival, or marketing event. The trophies invariably lead to questions and conversations. Sometimes people have even asked me if I am a trophy vendor! Regardless of the question, once

they stop and ask any question or initiate any conversation, we have the opportunity to build relationships. Often people will buy something from us simply because of the connection or relationship!

I immediately produced a new Virtual Background for my Conversations with #DrCybersecurity show! Once again, every earned media marketing opportunity must be milked for prolonged value to our brand!

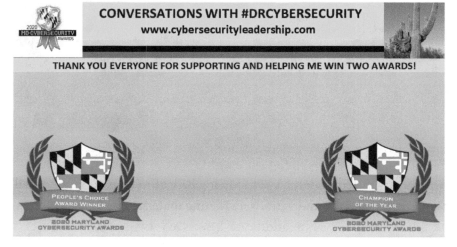

The following video https://youtu.be/o6_7BFHWaFQ from a portion of the proceedings, my introduction, and the video of my song had incredible impact! The number of commendations I received for this celebration video was simply amazing. Once again, my extra effort and being willing to change the game worked in my favor. Everyone will remember what I did for quite some time! You too must be willing to do things like that.

Recording Celebration Video for CAMI Awards 2020 in Case of Win!

After the event, organizers provided all winners a press release template. I used it and created a rich multimedia blog on LinkedIn and also sent it out to as many media contacts as I could. Even if the press release is not published by any media, my own blog, which was also posted on Twitter will continue to promote my personal brand for an exceptionally long time. In addition, my name will appear on the winners list on the host website.

These wins were even more important because at the time of the wins, I had disassociated myself from all organizational brands and simply competed on the strength of my own personal brand. Even on the listing for the contest and the portal for voting, my name was the only name that had no organization associated with it. Yet, I won two awards including a globally contested vote with the highest number of votes ever cast in that contest! That is what true independence from organizational brands means!

Such brand independence means that organizations benefit and gain value from our activities and successes far more than we do. Of course, these wins are likely to lead to a few more opportunities for me. They may lead to a few more book sales. However, if I had been associated with any university at the time of these wins, that university would have gained hundreds and possibly thousands of students, which would have resulted in multi-million dollar revenues and increased credibility for the university programs!

When anyone from a university wins an award or appears in any conference or media piece as a presenter or an interviewee, all programs, and the entire university benefits. I knew this and could see it in action. Even though I was associated with one cybersecurity program, all cybersecurity programs benefited with increased enrollment! Other programs at the university also saw increased enrollment.

In the modern world of student recruitment, ads do not bring in students - personal brands do! Ads may help a university gain some name recognition. However, in my experience it is an extremely high cost initiative with dubious returns. Universities with academic reputations do not advertise!

Therefore, ads frequently make even a non-profit university appear to be a for-profit university. Instead, earned media, which is free, is powerful. That can only be achieved through personal brands. We must make news to be in the news!

We must also maintain strong relationships with journalists and media personalities. They will frequently need to talk to experts for stories. These earned media mentions are powerful. Interviews on TV are powerful. We must recognize the value we add and not be willing to be exploited! Our personal brands are revenue engines for any organizations we choose to associate with. Do not ever lose sight of that!

8.11 GIZMOS

During my adventures in marketing and personal brand development, I had to try various technologies to produce high quality audio and video. While we can produce videos on our smartphones and tablets, I found that the following inexpensive gadgets and free software dramatically improved the quality of the final products.

1. Smartphone Video Rig: https://www.amazon.com/gp/product/B076FQCWQG

This gadget allows more stability while taking videos. It can be used as a handheld video rig or connected to a tripod with mounted light or additional accessories.

2. Tablet Holder for Tripod: https://www.amazon.com/gp/product/B07QFPSQ2H

   This holder allows me to mount a tablet directly on a tripod or on top of my Video Rig so it can serve as a teleprompter. The iPad has a free application called Pages, which can be used as a teleprompter.

3. Smartphone Mount for Tripod: https://www.amazon.com/gp/product/B072KNBV21

   This little gadget allows me to put the Smartphone on a table or a flat surface to take selfies or videos. I can also use it to mount the smartphone on a tripod.

4. Prograde Lavalier Lapel Microphones: https://www.amazon.com/gp/product/B07CHCSLVC

   These wonderful microphones connect to a smartphone input and will dramatically enhance the quality of the audio. They also allow two people to do an interview or simply talk about a topic.

5. Tripod: https://www.amazon.com/AmazonBasics-60-Inch-Lightweight-Tripod-Bag/dp/B005KP473Q

   This is an inexpensive tripod. Make sure your tripod allows you to change angle, height, rotation, and up and down movement of the camera.

6. USB Condenser Microphone: https://www.amazon.com/gp/product/B07GQT8879

   Condenser microphones are extremely sensitive and can dramatically improve voice recordings. After trying several, I settled on this one for clear warm sound and appropriate for picking up a single person speaking during a podcast or video meeting. Some microphones produced noise and required high noise cancellation, which reduced the quality of the vocals. This one improved my sound transmission at a reasonable cost for condenser microphones and it can be mounted on a wide range of microphone stands. In general, I found older MacBook Air and Pro laptops have decent microphone pickups. Recently, I tried a new 2020 MacBook Air and experienced constant overheating problems during my podcasts and had to return it. I tried a Dell Inspiron but could not get decent sound using the built-in microphone. The Windows 10 environment has not been very stable either. You may have to talk to many people and try several laptops to get the right laptop for podcasts and high quality recording. Finally, Apple's new iMac with their proprietary M1 chip, 1024p camera, and high quality sound worked well for recording purposes.

7. Bluetooth   Clicker: https://www.amazon.com/gp/product/B08526TB92

This Bluetooth clicker came free with the selfie stick and worked well with no delays. The selfie stick and stand are fragile. So, we must be careful. However, it is very portable and useful during travel or a hike.

8. Lighting: Lighting is extremely important, and you may need to buy something if you wish to make professional quality videos. I was able to get away with overhead lighting and table lamps. Some people use a circle light with great results.

9. Computer   Speakers   with   Subwoofer: https://www.amazon.com/Klipsch-Pro-Media-Certified-Speakers/dp/B009L1NY0M

I love this set of speakers in my setup as they do not produce any additional interference or noise and produce an exceedingly high quality sound. I was able to get a set from Costco on sale for $99 and they dramatically improved my music, video, and online meeting experiences. There are separate volume controls for the subwoofer and the satellite speakers. They are also excellent for playing MP3 music files while working on the laptop.

10. Audacity   Audio   Editing   Software: https://www.audacityteam.org/

I used this free open source software to produce my audiobook.

It is excellent for editing audio files. While downloading any software, make sure you are downloading from the official project site.

11. Shotcut Video Editing Software: https://shotcut.org/
I love this free open source video editing software. It has all kinds of powerful features, and I can separate out the audio and video tracks and edit them independently. I can also replace the audio track and add in music as needed. Of course, make sure you are using public domain or Creative Commons music.

12. Virtual Backgrounds. While Virtual Backgrounds are not gadgets by themselves, any video conferencing software lacking this feature is seriously deficient. Virtual Backgrounds can create an amazing effect for video podcasts and interviews. In addition, we can display website addresses, sponsor logos, and other marketing materials subtly.

We can create effects as well as use them as props during a presentation. I typically use a large assortment of Virtual Backgrounds depending on the venue and the subject. For Toastmasters meetings, I even use Green, Yellow, and Red Virtual Backgrounds as timing cards.

8.12 EDUCATION: HELP BRING INNER GREATNESS OUT

Education has a major role in helping everyone bring their inner greatness out. I believe we need a major overhaul in education so everyone has a chance at finding their passion and mission in life. Having taught first grade, third grade, fifth grade, traditional undergraduates, and working adult graduate and undergraduate students, I succeeded in bringing out the inner greatness in all my students who were willing to work with me.

I start by assuming they have inner greatness. I never assume some students will fail. I also think grading on a curve is unethical. Every student should get the grade they earned. Students in a class should never be made to compete against each other. Instead, they should be taught to collaboratively succeed.

While others teach every student in the same manner, I always treat each student as an individual and try to figure out how to help each student to learn and excel. I feel that the same approach can never work for every student because no two students are the same.

I also feel that different students may take different lengths of time to excel. However, most education systems I am familiar with, are not designed to cater to individuals. These systems target an average and set an expectation using some arbitrary standards, which do not consider the varying socio-economic or cultural factors that students are burdened with.

Automated testing systems are designed for efficiency and ease of grading for professors. In general, they do not accurately test student competencies. Students often do not perform well on tests because of stress. Stress triggers an amygdala hijack condition causing the brain to function at a far lesser capacity than it is normally capable of.

I also feel berating or punishing a student rarely works and can cause the opposite effect. When I show care and empathy for a student and the student feels I am on their side and genuinely interested in their success, the student bonds with me. Once this bond of trust is established, I can be a more effective teacher. Without this trust, no student will ever feel comfortable sharing their vulnerabilities with me. Bringing out inner greatness requires mentees to trust the mentor.

When I joined as a brand new teacher in first grade, just after completing my own high school, I had no one except my own natural instincts and beliefs to guide me. I believe that something special exists in everyone. A teacher's job is to help a student find it, nourish it, believe in it, and focus on it.

If they are unable to focus on their own greatness, they will get into trouble and lose sight of their real purpose in life. The sooner I can help a student find their inner greatness, the sooner I can get all of us to pull in the same direction.

During my time as a teacher in an international elementary school, I had the greatest challenge with two students. One was an American boy named Damon who had a reputation for bullying other students and getting into fights. Damon was very boisterous and naughty and immediately told me he did not like me. The other was a Burmese boy named Min.

I had learned from my own mother that the way to a child's heart was through love and care. We must earn the child's trust before applying any principles of discipline. A child is much more likely to listen to a person they trust.

I had already decided I was going to love every child in my class and do my best to help them to learn. I took Damon out of the class and started to talk to him. "You know something Damon – you are a very naughty child," I said very softly with a smile.

I saw that he was expecting these words from me – this is what every other teacher had given him. I also think he expected me to continue my conversation by giving him a stern lecture about how I expected him to behave. What he was not expecting was my smile or soft loving tone.

"You are a naughty, naughty boy, "I continued "but you know what? I love (with a lot of stress) naughty boys – I absolutely love naughty boys!" – That took him aback and I could tell he was not expecting this. Damon looked puzzled and shouted, "You are lying. No one likes naughty boys!"

"Oh no Damon – no way – naughty boys are very interesting – they are very intelligent; they are very curious – they are always trying to find out what to do next. Naughty boys have a lot of energy. I think I was a naughty boy too. I love naughty boys, and I really like you," I replied.

Damon was a bit more interested in our conversation now and he was indeed intrigued, "Why do you like naughty boys?" "Because naughty boys can do their work faster than anybody else and then after they finish their work they can have more time to play in the sand box or do other things – if I let you play in the sandbox or go out exploring don't you think you could finish your work faster than anyone else?" I asked.

"Yes, I can do my work faster than anyone else!" Damon was emphatic. Damon and I established our secret deal – if he finished his work faster than anyone else, he would get extra time to get out of the class and play in the sand box or explore. Since we had two teachers in this classroom, I offered to go with him to help him explore.

This approach worked wonders for Damon. We got our confirmation that our work with Damon had succeeded when his mother came over to talk to me at our next Parent-Teacher meeting. She was overjoyed –"Mr. Mansur I do not know what you have done but Damon has never enjoyed school as much as he enjoys it now – he used to get into fights with everyone else and now he is a very happy child."

I told her that I felt she had a highly intelligent son. I felt her son was getting bored and restless just sitting in class after finishing his work. While that workload was okay for others, Damon needed extra stuff to occupy his attention. Hence we had to devise a method to provide him more ways to release his energy and to satisfy his curiosity.

Min's situation was a little different. He was not doing his work because he seemed more interested in drawing and painting. I decided to give him all the time to paint and draw as soon as he finished his assignments. This approach worked well with him and soon he became a happy child also. His mother was so happy with our teaching method that she came to school to meet with us also.

Meeting Min's mother, who happened to be the wife of the Burmese Ambassador to Bangladesh at that time, was another major pivot point in my life! She mentioned that she was incredibly happy with Green Herald International School. She wanted to know what we could do for some new Burmese students who had just arrived in Dhaka.

These children had been studying in Burma (now called Myanmar) in their own language. However, without remedial coaching in English, they would not succeed studying in Grades Three or Five at our school. I knew I could provide this special coaching. So, I suggested she send the parents of the children to see Principal Sister Imelda. Surely we would find a solution.

Sister Imelda's solution was to let me tutor all these students in remedial English at the school premises during the afternoons. She told me she would not charge me any money and I could deal directly with the parents and charge my own rates. She even suggested a rate I should charge.

Suddenly, my income from private tutoring became five times my salary as a full time teacher! Everything happened simply because I had paid special attention to a special child! On top of that, teaching remedial English to several students from various grade levels in the same class, taught me that it is possible to give special attention to every student according to their needs.

This profound lesson early in my professional life sealed the idea in my mind that we must treat each student individually. It was the right way to teach; students in the same class should be allowed to learn at different paces. We should focus on the outcome and not the number of attempts. Giving every student a single attempt at any project did not make sense to me. Just because someone takes a little extra time or needs an extra attempt, it does not mean they are bad students or deserve a lower grade! Real professional life is not a timed automatically scored quiz.

When I joined UMUC as Program Chair of the graduate Cybersecurity Technology program in April of 2016, I found a unique opportunity to practically demonstrate my thinking that there is greatness within everyone; I had the opportunity to design a new program to do exactly that at a global scale with several thousand students. On top of that, I could do it without artificial gatekeepers.

By law, UMUC is an open university. That means it cannot have too many barriers to admission. For me, lack of barriers was absolutely refreshing as I never believed in preventing people from reaching their potential. I never saw a logical reason to use SAT or GRE scores and other means to predict how anyone will succeed in college!

I had taken all these tests and gone through these gatekeepers. I still remember that I did poorly in my LSAT exams because I never slept the night before and had to travel four hours in the morning to a different city using public transportation just to take the test. My brain was mush throughout the test. I did better in the SAT and GRE tests because I was rested. However, giving so much importance to these tests despite lengthy solid academic records made no sense. In addition, I always thought accomplishments outside the classroom are particularly important.

Many students are late bloomers. Many have challenging circumstances in their homes. Many have financial issues. Many fail in high school or lower levels because no one cared for them or gave them individual attention. The best way to find out if someone can succeed in college is by allowing them to join. Screening them out before giving them the opportunity makes no sense to me.

Having worked within the University System of Maryland for more than a decade before joining UMUC, I knew many other universities viewed UMUC as the university of last resort for students and therefore denigrated the institution for not having too many admission gatekeepers. I felt that the absence of artificial gatekeeping practices should be considered a strength - specially to ensure fair access to high quality education for all. This would help the university achieve better diversity and inclusion.

Every other university, however, appeared to pride themselves by how many students they turned down. Accepting a small percentage of students appeared to be a badge of honor for almost all universities. To me this does not make academic or fiscal sense. I even saw universities bragging about how difficult it is to graduate from their programs!

These barriers to higher education are often arbitrary and capricious and likely to give unfair advantage to wealthy and privileged families. If a university is already preselecting the so-called "cream of the crop," how can the university claim to have a role in their success? Furthermore, even after picking the "cream of the crop," if they cannot help students to graduate, how can they call themselves a high quality university? I found this culture of hubris at many "elite" universities to be very disturbing.

I feel the reputation of an institution should depend on its academic leadership as well as the teaching model and strategy. For me, what a graduate can do has always been far more important than what they know. Knowledge in most fields changes so rapidly that I had been an early proponent of competency-based education and had implemented this teaching model in all courses and programs I designed from the very beginning of my transition to academia.

I decided to take the opportunity at UMUC as my personal mission to build the world's finest graduate cybersecurity education program. I was thrilled to be able to try this at a large scale. I knew that the global demand was so high and the supply of programs so low that if I focused on quality and reputation, I would bring in thousands of students from all over the world and quickly become a monopoly supplier.

I knew the competition and I was unwilling to compete on price; I wanted to compete strictly on value. I knew lowering the tuition too much would trigger larger class sizes and lower faculty compensation. Without a cadre of top notch caring faculty with experiences in the field, I would not be able to implement my vision; the faculty must be able to give individual attention to every student. I wanted to build a culture of teaching excellence among the faculty.

I was not willing to support any decision that would result in a lower quality education. My stance was not always congruent with the constantly changing executive leadership above me who were more interested in maximizing numbers on a spreadsheet by reducing "expenses" on faculty without recognizing that faculty bring in the revenue and are not "expenses". I stayed true to my values and did not allow efforts to water down the education during my tenure.

I also noted that the word "online" had become synonymous with low quality because of the implementation at many educational institutions. I was unwilling to highlight this as a competitive advantage. It was easy for me to see that as more institutions implemented online education as a means of fiscal survival, this competitive advantage would be nullified. Furthermore, if students and graduates feel they received a lower quality education, they would be at a serious competitive disadvantage during their job searches.

I wanted my graduates to wear their degrees as a badge of honor. Thus, my message was consistent: We are the best program in the world; mode of instruction is immaterial since we provide the option of hybrid face to face classes as well. In 2017, after my program became the only academic program to receive an award from (ISC)^2 I told students and graduates to mention they were in an award winning program. My entire global social media network and their networks celebrated this accomplishment!

My focus was on quality and not on the mode of instruction. This is what I told students, prospective students, faculty, staff, and members of the public. I also engaged and trained the marketing and enrollment staff on this messaging to the extent I could get them to listen. After the program won back to back Best Cybersecurity Higher Education Program awards in 2018 and 2019 from SC Magazine, the quality and reputation of the program became indisputable globally!

I was unapologetic about my confidence that my graduate program was the best in the world. I remember one time a prospective graduate student asked me which professor's cybersecurity class at Harvard University he should take. Indignantly I asked him, "Have their programs or faculty won any national or international awards in cybersecurity? As Chair of the best graduate cybersecurity program in the world, it is difficult for me to suggest another university.

Why not do some searches for well-known cybersecurity professors and examine which university names come up? Do they have anyone with major contributions to the cybersecurity field? Are they invited to speak at conferences? Which university names do you see on cybersecurity conference agendas? Do these professors have work experiences in the field? Have they been a Chief Information Officer or a Chief Information Security Officer? What fields are their degrees in?

Book knowledge is not enough. Our field is an applied discipline and learning from someone who has never worked in the field will leave you highly deficient. You will need to know how to use your knowledge in the service of an organizational mission. Just because a university has an overall reputation, it does not mean they are the best in every field."

I explained that I did not come to education to make money. In fact, my compensation was far below what I used to make as a Chief Information Officer. My mission at this point in my life was to build the next generation of top notch digital strategists of the world and I had sincerely designed a program to do just that.

We had eliminated textbooks because most were obsolete and expensive. Instead, we used disaggregated curated learning materials at the topic level. This made us nimble; I was able to change content every term to keep it current. Sometimes, I had to change content in the middle of the term. If they wished to study cybersecurity in the best program in the world, they should join my program.

Ours was probably the only program where anyone from any field could join. In fact, only 22% of the 5,000 students globally in my graduate cybersecurity program came from previous computer, networking, or cybersecurity fields. 78% of the students came from social sciences, law, business, political science, math, history, and various disciplines. Many had taken time out of the traditional workforce to raise families for a decade! Half of the students were in the armed forces, and actively deployed; a large number were raising families and studying at the same time.

If they wanted to study in a cheaper program or a more expensive Ivy League university for other reasons that is fine. However, students joining our program should come with the idea that they will be future organizational leaders and my team, and I would do everything within our power to make their dreams come true. Their previous backgrounds did not matter. We cared about their destination.

The strategy worked dramatically well! Letting the students know up front they were in the world's best program gave them a high standard to look up to. It gave them confidence to focus on the work. I explained to them that the graduate education program I designed would make them the leaders modern organizations need. They simply needed to focus on the work and complete the program.

Within one year of program launch, I won the 2017 (ISC)^2 Information Security Leadership Award for implementing this groundbreaking academic program. Then, based on the following key features, the program won back to back Best Cybersecurity Higher Program in the USA Awards from SC Awards in 2018 and 2019.

- High quality practitioner scholar instruction globally in both 100% online and hybrid formats. Students would be told right up front that they are studying in the finest graduate cybersecurity program in the world. Setting up this expectation would help them rise to the occasion and visualize themselves in that greatness.
- Entire Cybersecurity Model permeating the program so students gain a solid foundation in the entire field.
- Multiple attempts for students to achieve mastery of competencies with actionable coaching and feedback from their instructors for each attempt.
- Principles of ethical leadership and focus on organizational mission as key values permeating the program.
- Students coached and mentored on personal success, networking, and perpetual learning.
- Faculty coached and mentored to deliver enhanced coaching and actionable feedback and make student success their focus and mission. I had noted a tendency for faculty to serve as judges rather than coaches. I changed this culture. I told my faculty that if a student is doing the work and still failing, faculty needs to investigate their own work and adjust. Only students unwilling to do the work according to the coaching should ever fail!
- Practical real world project focused education with no quizzes, tests, or discussions. Students would have to complete smaller scale versions of real world projects they will be expected to do in the real workplace. Their projects would incorporate leadership, teamwork, diversity, stakeholder communications, risk analysis,

and critical thinking. These would serve as examples of work they could take to their job interviews.

I marketed the program and the university using a global social media strategy, global thought leadership, and a global people network engagement. I judged that personal brand credibility would immediately give credibility to the program as well as the university and attract online students from all over the world. The program would be dramatically cheaper and convenient for international students.

When I revealed my goals and vision to several people, some were cynical about my vision. They told me that at an open admissions university I must accept the premise that half the students will fail! That was the history and I need to adjust my thinking.

Having never been defined by the past, I felt that this attitude did not make financial or academic sense. Since all admitted students had earned at least a Bachelor's degree, I saw no reason for them to fail if we took care of them academically and catered to them individually. I chose to ignore their warning.

When a student enrolls, we have the moral obligation to do everything within our power to help the student succeed. I feel spending energy and money on academics and retention is far more important than spending money on marketing and enrollment. Student success would automatically drive more enrollments.

I felt that we needed to work harder on that half who might drop out and perhaps we might succeed in retaining 75% or more. I feel we have a moral obligation to serve every student who has already enrolled and should not assume that half will not make it. I felt students were dropping because we were not taking care of them during the first class; I talked with many of them and they told me their reasons!

The first class in the graduate cybersecurity program was designed and run outside the cybersecurity department by non-cybersecurity professionals. I felt this course had serious issues both in content and administration. This is where we lost most of the students. I felt this class was the key to finding the exact weaknesses of each student. Simply using this class as a gatekeeper for subsequent classes made no sense to me.

However, I had to focus on things within my control. I focused on student success in all courses under my jurisdiction. I leveraged my own knowledge of technology, which now allows anyone to have meaningful professional relationships with thousands of people - specially students - globally. This engagement would serve as my best gage of the success of the program; I would learn quickly about any fine tuning I needed to implement.

Students, graduates, and prospective students would also have a direct line of communications with me. They would learn about the power of modern technology to run global companies; they would embrace digital strategy and perpetual innovation in their professional and personal lives. I also encouraged students and graduates to attend and network at conferences.

This would not only help me build professional mentoring relationships with students and graduates, it would also help them to build strong professional networks, which would be instrumental for their career success. I also negotiated free attendance at conferences for students.

I set up display tables at conferences to showcase our various awards and talk with prospective students and members of the public. I wanted them to know these awards were real and prestigious! I took pictures with students and the awards because I wanted the students to visualize themselves with those awards.

Showing Katia Dean and Tomiko Evans the (ISC)2 ISLA Award at
CyberMaryland 2017

The picture taken during CyberMaryland 2017 became historic three years later, after both Tomiko Evans and Katia Dean won (ISC)² Americas Information Security Global Leadership awards as Rising Stars in Cybersecurity in 2019 and 2020 respectively!

These global thought leadership and engagement activities provided results beyond my wildest dreams. During 2017-2018, my program experienced between 58%-69% annual growth rates in enrollment for students. Such levels of growth are unprecedented and far surpassed the growth rate for the entire university graduate school or other programs.

Student success and satisfaction went up. Faculty evaluation scores went up. My faculty started to win student nominated teaching awards and were featured in a variety of forums. They also received speaking invitations. Graduates started to become well known in the field globally.

During 2018, Tomiko Evans, who was part of the pioneer cohort in the innovative graduate program I had launched in the Fall of 2016, sent me a poem she had written explaining cybersecurity using the definition and teachings in my program. I noted that the poem appeared to have excellent rhythm and rhyme and explained the cybersecurity model well.

So, I suggested she turn it into a CyberRap. Within a few weeks, Tomiko produced a CyberRap. I then suggested that she open a conference presentation by singing this CyberRap with music and dance. Tomiko hesitated initially and wondered what others would think.

Although this reaction is natural and common, I also saw this reaction as a common example of the very thing that prevents people from bringing out their inner greatness - worrying about what other people will think. Societal pressure to conform is so strong that it creates a gripping paralysis that prevents people from showing the world all that they are capable of.

Yet, each person is unique. Therefore, greatness can only be achieved by setting that uniqueness free. People need to flaunt their uniqueness because no one becomes great simply by doing what others have already done. *They must do what has never been done before!*

In Tomiko Evans, I saw an inner greatness that was waiting to be liberated. She just needed to let go of her fears of what other people will think and simply embrace who she is and let that person out. She simply needed to package that inner greatness in her own way and let the chips fall where they may. Instead of trying to be anyone else, she needed to be herself with abandon! I also explained how greatness is a journey.

I explained to Tomiko how I never enjoyed doing anything others had already done; there is no fun in that. My entire career was built on doing what had never been done before. I also never worried about what others were going to say. Innovation always produces passionate and often powerful detractors. Sometimes the detractors can shut us down temporarily.

If that happens we must pivot to something else. However, we can never let others define us, or suppress our greatness. I explained we can never please everyone. Since the cybersecurity field requires perpetual innovation, she must continuously think of innovative things to do.

Through such innovation, she will establish her personal brand and take her rightful place in the field.

Finally, after six months of solid preparation, at the 2019 (ISC)^2 Secure Summit held in DC, Tomiko Evans created history by daring to open her presentation with a three minute rendition of Planes, Trains, Automobiles - complete with a music and dance routine. She followed it up with the fascinating story of her journey into the field and finding a mentor. She then explained the issues around drone security and, just for good measure, hacked a drone in midair and kept the audience riveted throughout her historic presentation.

She received a standing ovation within three minutes of hopping off the stage and climbing back on after dancing throughout the packed room while performing her CyberRap. She received another ovation in the middle of her presentation after the drone hack demonstration. The presentation was humorous, lively, educational, and completely different from any other presentation at the event!

As a matter of fact, a presentation like this had never been made at any cybersecurity conference before. Tomiko Evans had just established her personal brand and her place as a star in the cybersecurity field. #CyberRapper became synonymous with Tomiko Evans just as #DrCybersecurity had become synonymous with me.

The next day, the entire Secure Summit DC conference buzzed about her magical and innovative presentation. The (ISC)^2 leadership felt that someone like Tomiko Evans could be instrumental in bringing youth and energy to their conferences. They invited Tomiko Evans to do her CyberRap routine and speak at the (ISC)^2 National Congress in Florida - all expenses paid.

Since I had also taken a diverse contingent of thirty students for free to this event, after looking at the photos, one of my friends commented, "well you just pulled off the civil rights movement of cybersecurity conferences!" Strangely enough, I was not consciously doing anything. I was simply making sure the opportunity was available to all. Diverse representation occurred organically since my program had roughly 69% "minority" students - a term that has always made me cringe!

When I was invited to deliver the opening keynote at ARMA 2019 in Nashville, I was also provided with several free tickets. Matthew Nicklin, another graduate from my program, and Tomiko Evans took advantage of these free tickets and both made the effort to show up. By showing up here, Tomiko Evans got another opportunity for an amazing display of situational awareness and leadership.

About thirty minutes into my forty five minute presentation, the sound system failed. While waiting for the issue to be fixed, I bantered with the audience to keep them entertained. During my banter, I softly suggested perhaps the #CyberRapper may be willing to sing.

Tomiko Evans quickly volunteered, "I will read a poem." She then jumped on stage and performed her CyberRap in front of 1,200 people! Even though she was on stage a little over three minutes, her performance was flawless, innovative, and memorable. The opportunity came and she seized it! The audience went wild! We were both mobbed as we stepped off the stage! Many people thought we had planned it.

Tomiko Evans Dared to Wow 1,200 ARMA 2019 Attendees at Nashville with Her Impromptu CyberRap After the Sound System Failed During My Opening Keynote!

Soon we learned she won the (ISC)² 2019 Information Security Leadership Award for the Americas in the Up and Coming Professional of the Year category. As Tomiko's nominator and mentor, I also received an invitation to watch her win the award. Suddenly, the entire chain of command between me and the President of the university was replaced.

My new supervision eliminated all our travel funds. Without hesitation, I flew to Florida at my own expense, to attend the (ISC)² National Congress for one day and then attend the awards ceremony in the evening. There was no way I could miss this priceless event. The pictures and memories were unbelievable! I also met many amazing people in our field including many faculty teaching on my team.

Posters with Tomiko Evans' Name as a 2019 Award Winner!

The awards dinner and the ceremony were fabulous. I had taken a guitar strap for Tomiko assuming they would present her with an electric guitar like they had in prior years. However, this time they did not. They did give her a nice trophy and we all had a grand time taking pictures and creating unforgettable memories. The rest is history.

Once again, Tomiko Evans performed her signature CyberRap routine before her presentation. Her mom had a proud day watching Tomiko perform and win the 2019 Up-and-Coming Professional of the Year Award for the Americas! Her brand had just become stronger!

With Tomiko Evans, Winner of (ISC)2 2019 Up and Coming Professional of the Year

In 2020, another one of my graduates and mentees from the same pioneer class named Katia Dean won the (ISC)² 2020 Global Rising Star of the Year Award. This happened just three years after she and Tomiko

Evans attended their first major cybersecurity conference - CyberMaryland 2017 - and we took a picture together with my (ISC)² trophy!

Katia Dean with the 2020 Rising Star of the Year Award from (ISC)2 in the Global Achievement Awards for the Americas

I had encouraged both of them to attend conferences and apply to speak. I had also encouraged them to write. Even if they did not wish to get published, I encouraged them to write articles on LinkedIn or on their own websites. By sharing their knowledge, they would not only refine their knowledge, they would also build their personal brands and become leaders in the field.

Immediately after graduation, as she pursued her own professional success, Katia Dean started to help others transition into the field and created a website called https://katiascylife.tech/ for this purpose. On her site, she shared her own learning and journey into the field and established a business helping people from a wide range of disciplines understand how their previous experiences were relevant in the cybersecurity field.

Her website is a master class for anyone's job search journey. Katia was not simply looking for a job. She was firing on multiple cylinders and had a clear focus on what she wanted and how all her experiences and education translated to make her best qualified. She also learned how to explain and define cybersecurity properly.

She mastered the NICE/NIST job roles framework and honed her ability to talk about it in simple terms. Throughout the entire time, as she continued learning, teaching, and helping others, her business, leadership profile, and the value of her personal brand, kept growing. Her personal brand spoke for her well before she showed up for job interviews. Such projection of personal brand value also translated into a stronger negotiating position for higher salary offers. Prospective employers could obviously see that someone with her profile was likely to be in high demand.

However, she did not stop investing in her personal brand after finding a job - the pursuit of greatness never ends with a job because the job should not define the person. She firmly established her personal brand as the #VoiceOfCyberPros. She continued her mission to help others transition and find jobs in the field.

She was interviewed multiple times. She coached recruiters once she recognized how broken the hiring system is. She explained that cybersecurity is not simply about hackers. She also explained the various paths into the field. She took her mission on the road by setting up tables at conferences and volunteering to help conference attendees with career and resume advice.

Adjacent Conference Display Tables With Katia Dean, 2020

At the Blacks in Cybersecurity Winter 2020 Conference we both wore our personally branded shirts and exhibited at adjacent tables! We networked with all the attendees - many of whom we met in person for the first time! It was a proud moment for all of us. Then on March 4, 2020, on a whim, I felt she was ready to write her book. So, I planted the seed and sent her the following message:

MAR 4

 Dr. Mansur Hasib, CISSP, PMP, CPHIMS · 2:00 PM
Almost seems like you ought to be publishing a book soon from all your blogs etc - including stories about resumes, job hunting, interviewing etc. Without names of people of course.

Message to Katia Dean

I thought she might take a year or so to complete the project. Nope. As her Program Chair, I had observed her finishing eleven weeks' worth of class work in seven to eight weeks. After that, she used to spend the rest of the term coaching her classmates. Therefore, just a few weeks later, she not only produced the book but started to market and sell it. She even coaxed several people, including me, to contribute their own stories about transitioning into cybersecurity within an overly aggressive deadline.

She embraced her own humorous "comic relief" personality and brought this out during her numerous conference presentations, and used her wit, humor, and quips to soften the constructive criticism she provided on every resume she analyzed. Even I volunteered my resume for one of her public resume analysis sessions.

She found numerous issues in my resume and pointed them out. However, because of her style of talking, at no time did I feel offended. Every issue she identified was actionable and true and if I changed them, my resume would improve dramatically. At the end of her analysis I jokingly wondered out loud how I landed a job with all those issues in my resume.

Katia Dean is currently having a lot of fun producing comic strips related to people finding jobs in cybersecurity. These comics are enjoyable to read and very catchy. She has incorporated these into her conference presentations and is a sought after speaker at various conferences across the globe! Katia has embraced herself, let her inner greatness out, and has established a compelling global personal brand!

Both Tomiko Evans and Katia Dean developed into who they are today only because they used all the principles I have shared in this book and dared to let their inner greatness out. Such inner greatness exists in everyone. Countless other graduates from my classes have done so. The key is to show up and dare to let it out. Greatness is a choice.

8.13 SUCCESS IS A TEAM SPORT

As the strength of our brand grows, it is critically important for us to help our team members grow their personal brands as well. Success is a team sport. We can never succeed within a losing team. By uplifting everyone on our team, we will multiply our greatness exponentially. We can amplify our greatness further by expanding the circles of people in our organization we can lift up.

This type of pervasive leadership culture is powerful in any organization and we can foster such a culture by practicing and teaching a set of values. These values can form the dominant culture of the organization. I have already shared my preferred set of values earlier in the book.

During my job interview at UMUC, I was asked the question almost everyone is asked at any job interview: "Why should we hire you? Why are you the best candidate?" My response was, "I will never knowingly let any team member fail. I will work hard for the success of everyone around me." This is a unique response that has not only been true for my entire career, but also works very well during a job interview.

However, the response shares several things that are likely to please everyone in the room. Once a face to face interview has been scheduled, the qualifications are no longer in question. During the interview, everyone is wondering how a candidate will fit in and work with everyone else. Any candidate who does not address this concern will not be rated well. Therefore, when a candidate promises to help all other team members succeed, how can they turn that candidate down?

Thus, as promised during my job interview, immediately after winning the People's Choice Award in Cybersecurity in 2017, I worked hard and helped my then supervisor Dr. Emma Garrison-Alexander win the award in 2018. That same year I also helped my fellow Program Chair Dr. Patrick O'Guinn to win the 2018 Information Governance Expert of the Year award. I also helped the university win the 2018 Information Governance Service Provider of the Year Award.

Continuing the promise of helping everyone around me succeed, I spent many hours helping colleague Dr. Tamie Santiago with her doctoral dissertation process. I helped several colleagues prepare and submit successful conference presentation proposals which were accepted. I also mentored several research fellows transitioning into teaching cybersecurity.

In 2019, I helped another team member Dr. Loyce Pailen win the 2019 People's Choice Award in Cybersecurity. These wins and the campaigns that preceded the wins increased and strengthened my own personal brand due to the publicity; it also helped the organization.

Multiple winners on the team showed that our programs did not depend on just me. Helping others win promoted everyone's personal brands. It created goodwill and a stronger leadership team. This camaraderie, mutual respect, and collaborative harmony among the program academic leadership and team were also noted by the External Review Team during the 2019 Academic Program Review.

I also established strong relationships with the Career Services department and made countless introductions between hiring companies and Career Services. This allowed hiring companies to know about the strengths of the program and to gain access to students to talk to them about opportunities. We trained students in interview and networking techniques. We also integrated faculty, staff, and alumni as mentors for incoming and current students. These efforts dramatically increased the likelihood that students would find roles while as a student or soon after graduation.

These discussions with employers helped us continue to gage if our graduates were meeting their needs and alerted us to any improvements we would need to make. Amazingly enough, we learned time and time again that the communications and critical thinking skills of the graduates from my program were exceptional and off the charts compared to typical graduates they were meeting at other universities.

Building and maintaining relationships with Career Services dramatically helped both departments and ultimately both the employers and our students. We also learned each other's languages and ability to talk about the services in each department with prospective students and employers. I gained more confidence that reimagining and overhauling the academic program was a dramatically positive step for everyone.

The entire cycle of activities increased the prominence of the institutional brand as a high quality cybersecurity program in a wide range of ever growing circles. In my view, this became an excellent model of a modern university marketing strategy.

8.14 CHALLENGING THE BRAIN

The program I designed has a lot of work and requires a significant amount of time commitment and discipline for students. Without sufficient challenge, the brain will not experience the permanent intellectual growth a graduate program is supposed to deliver. This, of course means, many students will feel overwhelmed and either seek to reduce work or drop with a full refund. Thus, the first course required an extraordinary level of professor and program chair engagement. I always preferred to teach this course because it allowed me to get a student on the right track at the beginning - particularly if the student had come from an unrelated field and needed preparatory courses in order to succeed before continuing on in the highly intensive and fast-paced graduate program.

Thus, I made it a habit to offer a phone discussion immediately after the first project submission. These discussions helped me on three critical levels:

1. Understanding the student's baseline and how I might need to adjust my approach to help a particular student succeed.
2. Ensure the student is aware of all the success resources available from the university.
3. Learn and respond to any student concerns or questions about the program or their career goals in general.

During such a conversation, I noted a sense of resignation with a particular student named Daria Moaadel.

"I came to this country as a new bride and I have been a stay-at-home mom for the last ten years and my brain does not work anymore. My English is not good. I cannot do this program. I will drop out," stated my student.

"Since your brain has not been challenged in this way for the last ten years, it is normal for your brain to resist. Your brain will adjust and by the end of the term it will start to operate at a new level. Whenever you start an exercise routine, your whole body will ache. You can stop. However, if you keep exercising, your body will start to operate at a much more efficient level and the pain will go away. The change in your brain will be permanent," I promised.

I worked her through the first project and explained various approaches she could take to strengthen the project. I recommended that she work with the free Writing Center. Her writing was not that weak. I thought she would rise to the level required for success within a couple of terms. She needed to continue working the projects and not give up. After gaining an understanding of her pervious educational preparation, I recommended a series of preparatory courses, books, and training she should take before continuing on to the next course in the program.

I also helped her visualize her future. "If your dream is truly to be a cybersecurity professional, you are in the world's best program right now. Once you finish, you will be able to write your own ticket to success. You just need to do the work in the manner I have recommended. If you need three attempts you have that option. Our goal is for you to learn how to do these projects.

All your class projects will serve as artifacts for your job interviews. You can show them what you can do. This is a competency based program - not a memory based program. In this program you will learn teamwork, presentations, writing, and how to think like an executive and a leader in the field. Your brain will be changed forever in this program," I said.

Luckily, she did not drop from my course. She succeeded in my class and I never heard from her for several terms. Then just one term before her graduation, I got a message from her and this was our conversation chain:

Daria: "When I started the program, I was a stay at home mom of 10 years. Today I am in Capstone in Bruce's class and have a job in cyber. So proud and thankful!! I tell everyone how you stayed on the phone with me for an hour for project 1 when I wanted to drop out. Cheers."

Me: "Yes and I still remember that conversation. I am so thankful you believed and worked hard. I am sure you can see that your brain has now changed forever! This is the promise I made to you. Your story needs to be told as many people will be helped. I will start the introductions."

Daria: 700 students and you remember our phone call ? You did make a promise, I thought you were trying to sell the program and waste my parents money ?.

(Note: At that time, I had 4,800 students in the program.)

This degree did make a difference in a short time in my and my children's lives. As a single parent I try to inspire my daughters to believe and challenge themselves.

I intentionally was choosing the hybrid classes. In most classes I was the only girl. It wasn't easy but I got in the car and drove to Dorsey. I broke the fear of public speaking and will be happy to tell my story. Thank you for believing in me."

During my chat, with Daria Moaadel, I further learned that she had followed all my advice to take the series of preparatory courses and training I had outlined for her. Happily, during her A+ course, life also rewarded her with an unexpected gift - a man who became her study partner, best friend, and love! Today, she has a thriving career at a global consulting company and has periodically reached out to me to hire more of my students. Seeing her radiant confident smile at her graduation in 2019 was a particularly memorable moment of euphoria in my life!

Daria Moaadel Graduating with a Master of Science, 2019

I have always felt that there is a serious lack of credible high quality options for students who have to drop out of the workforce to raise a family or for other reasons; we need strong programs for anyone who wishes to transition careers or reenter the professional workforce after an absence. Therefore, saving this student and helping her to bring out her confidence and inner greatness, was particularly important for me.

However, this choice of greatness and the work required to get there, could only be made by her. She had to trust I was telling her the truth; she had to decide to continue to spend the money and do the work to challenge and retrain her brain to rise to a higher level of complexity, and with that, a much higher level of income. I also knew that this single success story would have a multi-generational impact for a young woman raising children and becoming a strong role model for her daughters! This is the type of individualized education we need instead of the current model of teaching to an average, where students who cannot succeed on their own in one attempt, are simply discarded without any realistic mentoring, coaching, or plan to help them succeed!

8.15 STUDENTS WITH SPECIAL ABILITIES

I have always disdained the terms "disabled" and "handicapped" because they are inherently derogatory terms, and they stigmatize people who are different. Our societal terms and practices relegate such people to diminished lives and possibilities. While we have created laws to provide some level of equal access for such people, we rarely seek to help them capitalize on their uniqueness.

One encounter with a blind graduate student who called me up for some career advice, reinforced my manner of thinking on this issue. He was lamenting his situation and wondering about his job prospects due to his "disability." He told me he appreciated my audiobook and perspective. After talking with him at length and realizing his passion for making a difference, I suggested he view his "disability" as a unique ability that very few people have.

While he cannot change his condition, he can change his way of thinking about it. "Only you can feel and know the world of someone who is blind. Have you thought about creating educational content relevant to others? Since you cannot change it, is it possible to think of it as one of your assets? You had to solve a lot of problems to join a graduate program in cybersecurity.

Could you create videos or even write books or audiobooks about your own story? Could you create videos explaining what you are learning about cybersecurity in a way that would help others in your situation and give us a better glimpse into your world? Why not use your unique situation as a strength and not view it as a weakness? Only you can do what I am suggesting. I certainly cannot ever express the same unique viewpoint you have!" At the end of the conversation, I felt I had succeeded in helping him develop a different point of view.

I have attended women's leadership events and suffered through hours of men bashing and hours of presentations explaining how women can be like men. Even books appear to focus on teaching women how to be like men. I have even seen women trying to be abrasive and cutthroat in the false assumption that it will allow them to fit in better and be successful.

My advice has always been simple: *Instead of playing someone else's game that is already rigged against you, change the game!* If you create a game only you can play, you will win every time. Why not make changing the game constantly a career strategy? That is what I have always done my entire life! It can be a success strategy for anyone!

Follow the systematic methodology and ideas shared in this book and carve your path to greatness!

8.16 BELIEF IS THE GENESIS OF SUCCESS

If you examine all the stories I shared, you will see that every success story starts with belief. They all believed I was telling them the truth. They trusted the information I provided. They believed they could achieve what I was asking of them. They believed they could succeed. Without believing they can succeed, no one can succeed.

8.16.1 Visualize the Future

My role was simply to plant the seed of greatness in each person's brain and to help them visualize their future. When people can visualize something, they believe it can be done. I helped them focus on the solution instead of focusing on the problem. That is why they succeeded.

8.16.2 See No Limitations

I also helped them understand that there are no limits to success. They can be the best in the world. If someone will be recognized as the best in the world, why not them? If I can get someone to believe they can be the best in the world, they can be the best in the world! That is the power of belief.

Countless stories can be found about this principle. The best example is in the field of running. For decades no one could run a mile under four minutes until Roger Bannister broke the 4-minute mile running barrier in 1954 by relentlessly visualizing this feat in his mind. After his success, since everyone knew this could be done, many others repeated the feat.

Once people find their greatness, and start their virtuous cycle of success, they go into autopilot. Greatness is intoxicating and rightfully so! We should celebrate our achievements. We should show others the way. Helping someone else succeed will never diminish our own success. Instead, our success will experience a multiplier effect when we help others succeed. That is the magic of leadership!

8.17 DOCUMENTATION

Maintaining the documentation of all your professional activities and accomplishments is just as important as the activities themselves. Create a system to maintain everything in an orderly format. In my case, I maintain an annual list of all the professional speaking engagements since 2017.

Since people will have a hard time finding them on LinkedIn or any other location, I have a page for Events on my website: https://www.cybersecurityleadership.com/about.html

On this page, I maintain links to events and speaking engagements organized by year. I update the speaking engagement page after the event to post videos, pictures, or news of the event. This makes it easier to find and include in any portfolio you may need to submit for promotions or personal brand enhancement.

The following are four years of my public speaking engagements. I maintain them in a publicly visible manner to ensure that they continue to promote my brand. I want them to be found in search results. I also point to them whenever anyone wants to see examples of my previous speeches and presentations:

2017

https://www.linkedin.com/pulse/september-2015-speaking-engagements-hasib-cissp-pmp-cphims/

2018

https://www.linkedin.com/pulse/2018-public-speaking-schedule-dr-mansur-hasib-cissp-pmp-cphims

2019

https://www.linkedin.com/pulse/2019-speaking-schedule-dr-mansur-hasib-cissp-pmp-cphims/

2020

https://www.linkedin.com/pulse/2020-speaking-events-schedule-dr-mansur-hasib-cissp-pmp-cphims/

2021

https://www.linkedin.com/pulse/2021-speaking-events-schedule-dr-mansur-hasib/

If you are wondering why I do not have the information organized so well before 2017, I simply did not think of it. As a matter of fact, I even made the mistake of revising the 2015 speaking list and reused it for 2016 and 2017! Do not repeat my mistake. Start right, and you will never lose track of all your accomplishments.

In addition, I have a YouTube Channel, and a rich website - all of which are important and interlinked. Each video on my channel has multiple keyword tags so that they will come up on YouTube searches and can be found easily by various streaming services. If you forget to add these tags, you can go back and add them back later to any video on your channel. You should also organize related videos into playlists.

You should also passionately solicit subscribers to your channel. If your channel is interesting and has useful content, people will subscribe because such subscriptions are free for now. At the time of this writing, once you have 1,000 subscribers, you will be able to monetize your videos through ads.

8.18 BIOS AND PROFESSIONAL PICTURES

Always have a richly written bio with human interest elements instead of a chronological bio with lots of facts and accomplishments. Give people some things so they can relate with you. In my case, I put in the fact that I have been to all 50 states of the USA. This little tidbit has caused many questions such as, "Which is your favorite state?" or "Ah, but how many provinces of Canada have you been to?" Always remember questions and conversations are the keys to building relationships!

Similarly, you can have a professional headshot, or you can have a picture that creates intrigue and begs some questions. One of my favorites is my picture with the $(ISC)^2$ Award guitar. That picture shares a story without any words being spoken. It has become synonymous with my brand and many people immediately started referring to me as the "Rock Star of Cybersecurity."

Similarly, I do not recommend unwelcoming poses such as ones with arms folded across the chest - a common pose preferred by photographers but conveys distance. Instead try open stances and you will be amazed! Whatever you choose to use, always have them ready to go as you will often be asked to provide them with little notice.

The faster you can provide them, the faster you will appear on the conference websites and your brand promotion will begin faster. Anytime you are speaking somewhere, make sure you promote the engagement - multiple times in as many social media platforms you are active in. Conference organizers love speakers who help promote the event.

Such activity will make you far more prominent than other speakers who may not be doing similar promotions. Your rise to greatness will be faster! Many people will come to a conference because of you. Ask for a registration code (preferably free or with a discount) so you can track your leads. Meeting these people at the conference will be fun for you and them.

Always remember that even if you do the greatest things, if no one knows about them, they are useless in terms of value creation or brand promotion for yourself. Knowledge is power. Let people know!

CHAPTER 9

How Can We Leverage and Protect a Personal Brand?

Once a strong personal brand has been established, it will speak for us well before we show up for any job interview and usually well before we are even invited for job interviews. Astute organizations will recognize the extent to which someone's personal brand may enhance the brand value of an organization or a program resulting in millions of dollars pouring in. In many cases, unsolicited lucrative job offers will come our way.

Even the simple news of a strong and credible personal brand name hire can result in instant recognition for an organization. Therefore, organizations spend money on press releases to announce such hires. Every time I associated my personal brand with a university, it immediately resulted in hundreds and even thousands of additional students. We must always remember that at the end of the day, we remain a free capitalistic economy.

In some cases, the revenue we generate is direct and clearly tangible and calculable. For example, at the time I joined UMUC, the program had roughly 1,500 students. By the time I left after roughly 3.5 years, the program had grown to roughly 4,800 students. After my departure, the program shrank dramatically.

In addition to direct tangible revenue in increased sales, we also generate lots of intangible and indirect sales that occur because of our brand promotion activities. My program grew from $30 million annual revenue to $117 million annual revenue. Of course, the marketing department may claim they were solely responsible for the increase since they had been spending multi-million dollars in ads, signs, and brand promotion of the university.

However, for a program that is more than ten years old and had never won any academic program awards in cybersecurity, could ads explain a dramatic enrollment increase of such magnitude during my tenure when ad spending and marketing personnel had declined during that same period?

Since each student represented $25,000 in total tuition revenue, I knew my documented annual revenue influx was between $1.7 to $2.5 million because I kept track of every direct student recruitment I facilitated. However, the outdated accounting system that every organization uses today does not account for the revenue and profits that every employee brings in. This is one area of improvement organizations need to make.

When I worked in a private company, the company kept track of the money I was bringing in and saving through renegotiations of contracts or licensing deals. So even though the company went through five rounds of layoffs during my tenure there, the people making the decisions always decided not to lay me off because they understood the layoff would result in several million dollars of losses and not save anything. My name did come up in every round of layoff decisions!

We must recognize our brand value in clear mathematical and financial terms and must leverage and negotiate compensation based on the value we generate and the money we will bring in and not on artificial budget numbers that every organization is now likely to throw our way.

No one cares about the budget when we are a revenue generator. We are not expenses. We are the profit centers of any sensible organization. It is best to associate with organizations that recognize this truth. If we enable the concept that we are expenses and enable unfair compensation to perpetuate, we will never achieve our true value.

9.1 RESUME AND LINKEDIN PROFILE

Now that you understand personal branding and how to discuss the value you bring to any position; you need to rethink how you write your resume and showcase yourself on business social media such as LinkedIn.

9.1.1 Resume

There are many excellent resources on YouTube and other websites about resumes. So, I am simply going to provide some tips here. In general resumes must be tailored to the industry, the specific job, and even the specific sector. For example, resumes for federal jobs tend to be dramatically different from private sector jobs. Academic resumes are also dramatically different.

There are several gatekeepers for resumes. First, you have automated systems that scan the resume for keywords and phrases that the job posting requested. If you tailor your resume to address the requirements of a job posting, you are more likely to get through this gatekeeper. If your resume gets to a human, you will typically have roughly eight seconds to catch the interest of the person. Make it easy for the person to understand your key strengths within those precious eight seconds. Your knowledge of personal branding should help you revamp your resume so that your personal brand and value stands out.

I try to convey a lot of information in my name itself and the way I display my terminal degree and major certifications as part of the name. Then I focus on the Summary. In this section, I use three or four sentences to capture the most relevant elements of my skills and experiences. I showcase results and accomplishments and use numbers. For example, saying I brought in $117 million revenue annually is far more powerful than saying I was responsible for running an academic program.

Address as many elements of the job requirements in your resume as possible by showing accomplishments in the areas listed in the job description. Do not worry about meeting 100% of the job requirements. If you think you can do the job, apply. You can never get the job you did not apply for!

Listing job responsibilities on a resume is weak. Instead list the accomplishments. How did you make a difference? How much difference did you make? Did you reduce spending by 10%? Did you increase revenues by 5% or 50%? Continue this type of theme throughout the entire resume.

When you list job positions you have held, consider whether to put the actual title or the functional title. For example, your title may say Senior Analyst. However, functionally you may be the Team Leader. Without fabricating anything, let the resume highlight your personal brand and how you made a difference in every role.

You should list speaking engagements, voluntary roles in organizations such as Toastmasters, as well as articles, interviews, news stories, awards, and other such information that highlight the range of your abilities. The wider your range, the higher value you are likely to represent to an organization.

9.1.2 LinkedIn

YouTube also has tons of great videos about how to create a strong LinkedIn profile. As I have stated before, LinkedIn is not simply an electronic resume. It is a medium for developing professional relationships and for showcasing your personal brand and accomplishments. I shared many of my insights in this YouTube Playlist: https://www.youtube.com/playlist?list=PLorvYEvhshhJBN0jL5-Xy-CBczmegef8_v

People use LinkedIn for a variety of purposes. I use the free version because I feel that without our content and presence LinkedIn has no value. Therefore, our presence and contributions alone are the reason LinkedIn can sell ads and stay a relevant forum. I feel LinkedIn should be providing a lot more services at no cost.

Read and follow the community rules and report people who harass or do not follow community rules. Do not harass people or make unprofessional comments. LinkedIn is not a dating site. Stay focused on projecting your professional personal brand and you should be fine. If you make an error because of a lapse of judgement, you can always edit or delete a post or a comment.

LinkedIn's Social Selling Index has four dimensions, which suggest the main areas this platform can help you with: 1) Establishing Personal Brand, 2) Finding the Right People, 3) Engaging with Insights, and 4) Building Relationships. You can get your score for free. You can periodically check your score on this index. Examine the movement in the scores. However, keep in mind that this index is primarily tuned for sales professionals.

My two primary goals have always been Building Relationships and Establishing Personal Brand. Therefore, my scores in those dimensions are more valuable to me than the other two. It is highly likely that their services are designed to improve your scores in certain categories.

My LinkedIn SSI on May 10, 2020

LinkedIn has also changed their interface, algorithm, and many features during this time. I do not suggest paying too much attention to the scores. However, being in the top 1% in your industry or your network may be important to you. This is one of the ways you can determine the effectiveness of your LinkedIn presence.

My LinkedIn SSI on August 18, 2021

As you can see, some minute movements in my scores occurred from May 2020 to August 2021. I am not sure why my scores are comparatively lower in two categories. I am also not sure why my professional brand score declined during the last 15 months when in reality my brand building activities have increased as has my educational content creation.

We must also remember that LinkedIn's primary goal is to get you to buy their paid services. Scores also compare you to your industry and your network. Thus, adding people with strong personal brands may lower your Network SSI rank even though the actual reach of your personal brand increased. These are all interesting insights. However, I do not recommend stressing over them.

You should also use LinkedIn to tell your network about your interesting professional activities. Most of all, you should be using it to share valuable content that you developed or found in your areas of interest. Such activities will help you to develop a community of supporters around your area of passion. One of the best ways to learn is by watching others who are doing it well. You are certainly welcome to follow my activities.

Recruiters and hiring managers are almost certain to look at your LinkedIn profile. If you have none, you will be at a serious disadvantage. If your LinkedIn profile is far less impressive than your resume, people will wonder why. Is it because your resume is inflated? Or is it because you do not use or know how to use LinkedIn? Either way, you will be hurting your chances.

Pay close attention to your LinkedIn headline, professional picture, summary, and all the accomplishments in each of your job roles. You should also collect recommendations from supervisors, professors, clients, colleagues, and display videos, certificates, articles, and other key artifacts that demonstrate evidence of the results you have produced.

If you send a connection request to someone you have not met, include a short note to provide the context or reason for seeking the connection. This will make it more likely that your connection request will be accepted. However, if you do not have a profile photo or a properly filled out LinkedIn profile, your connection request may not be accepted.

LinkedIn's Write Article feature is a great way to write content with a much longer shelf life. You can put in pictures, videos, and links to make an article come alive. You can always go back and edit these articles and even take them down when you feel they are no longer relevant. Blogs are a great way to start writing a book. Each blog could eventually become a chapter in a book.

You must use hashtags in every post to make them easier to find later. People do follow hashtags. Hashtags will allow you to find even your own posts many months or years later. In my case, #DrCybersecurity, #Cybersecurity, #Leadership, #GreatnessISaChoice, #RideTheRainbow, #CybersecurityLeadership, #CybersecurityEducation are examples of hashtags I use regularly and people following those hashtags will easily find my posts even if they do not use LinkedIn every day. While you can use about 30 hashtags in each post, do not go overboard on hashtags as the post will look messy.

While you can also tag people, in general it is highly inappropriate to tag someone simply to promote your post; such misuse may result in someone blocking you. Instead, engage with other people's posts and you will find that they will also engage in yours. I am constantly supporting posts from people who engage in my posts - unless it is a pure marketing post. That is the proper use of cross-brand promotion. If people are not reciprocating, you can also stop promoting their posts. If all your posts are about your company or product, you are unlikely to gain much engagement.

You may need to watch several free training videos on YouTube or attend training sessions to create a compelling LinkedIn profile. Just like growing a personal brand, learning to use social media is also a journey. However, in this modern world, if you want to express your greatness, you will need to embrace this journey. Anyone can do it.

9.2 COMPENSATION NEGOTIATING TIPS

Do not negotiate compensation based on needs, fairness, living conditions, inflation, or even cost of living. Instead, negotiate based on the revenue you generate. We must recognize and leverage the revenue we bring in. This type of argument will also lead to positive outcomes when asking for raises and promotions.

Negotiate with a smile. Do not ever feel insulted with low ball offers. Do not insult anyone. Always leave the ego aside. You can always counter with a similarly ridiculous offer to take a $0 salary in exchange for half of the revenue generated or expenses saved; do this with a smile. I have suggested this many times but have had no takers yet.

Your success at negotiating the right compensation or contract with a sliding performance based scale will be your first test if your main job is to negotiate deals. Always request a revisit if things are going nowhere. If your personal brand is strong, there is only one of you and plenty of organizations to choose from! Make them sweat.

Once they have made an offer, they are invested in the hire. They may be far more worried about losing you. So, acting coy and requesting a couple of weeks to think about it and discussing with family members are always great tactics. Always remember, if you have a strong personal brand you are the money maker, and they will need you far more than you will need them.

Research what other executives are making. Research public records for non-profit organizations at sites such as www.guidestar.org. Talk to contacts. Check various salary sites. However, above all make sure you extol your track record of revenue generation. Nothing speaks better than proven past performance.

9.3 STAY IN YOUR LANE

Once a personal brand is established it must be guarded zealously. A brand that has taken years to build can be lost in a moment of careless frenzy. Furthermore, once a strong brand value has been established, we will get a variety of requests to be associated with various initiatives. Many of these requests will come with no tangible financial benefits for us. However, they are likely to have huge financial benefits for the requestor.

Many of these requests will involve advisory board positions. If they are paid positions, we need to evaluate if the association is likely to have any negative impact on our personal brand. Organizations will use the names and personal brands of advisory board members to generate value and sales for their organizations. The key is for us to evaluate if such association will enhance or diminish our brands. This is not an easy assessment but must be done for every association request we receive.

Similarly, if we are business professionals, musical artists, or actors, engaging in public political or religious discussions may not be in our best business interests as they will invariably divide our customers, and many may never come back. Furthermore, enraged customers may be sufficiently upset to cause more reductions in sales.

I use a few key principles to leverage and protect my personal brand. Is the mission of the organization aligned with my mission? Will they be using my work, models, or books to promote their mission? If so, that might help me. However, if they will simply use my name and brand to give credibility for their work, my brand value and sales of my own work may suffer.

Criticizing politicians or people in government is usually not a great idea - specially if our profession is supposed to be apolitical and we are supposed to serve all. It is best to avoid religious topics as well. We may need to weigh in on social justice issues. Once again, while it can be appropriate if done with care, in general the danger of brand dilution and even damage can occur if we stray too far away from our lanes. Furthermore, our understanding of the issues may not be at the same expert level as our primary disciplines.

9.4 BE CAREFUL OF WHAT YOU ENDORSE

We must also assess if we are in support of the initiative we are being asked to promote. For example, if the mission is a certification program and our brand is all about higher education and university degrees, supporting a certification program may be incongruent with our personal brand. I was once a finalist for the Chair position for a new cybersecurity program at a major state university - except the university did not wish to offer degrees in cybersecurity.

"Our goal is to produce cybersecurity workers faster and there's a lot of money in offering certificate programs," they explained. "We already have selected the courses. Furthermore, we can offer the certification program without going through the accreditation process."

"Can this certificate program be on the way to a degree? I am willing to take a degree program through the accreditation process," I asked.

"No, it is too political. Many other departments will object to a new degree program because it might compete with their programs," they said, much to my astonishment. When I asked who had selected the course to be offered, I quickly found out that the people who made course selections had no education or experience in the cybersecurity field. They had simply adopted courses offered by various certification vendors.

I felt they were being unethical on many fronts. First, students would never know the certificate program was not enough to prepare them properly; they would trust the university to give them what they need to succeed. Even if the certificate resulted in a job, due to the lack of accreditation, the investment would never count towards a degree at most respectable universities; they would come out inadequately prepared. On top of that, most of the people who had selected the courses or might teach them would have no academic or practical backgrounds in cybersecurity. This important fact would be hidden from the public because the program would be front ended by me!

I felt lending my personal brand to such a program would not be ethical; I would lend credibility to the program and attract students, but they would come out unprepared - all while the university would make lots of money. "This program will be putting out a lot of unprepared students rather quickly! Neither the students nor their prospective employers would know this. I cannot see myself lending my brand to sell this program," I said, as their eyes grew wide in astonishment. They were rather surprised I would turn down such a lucrative salary.

None of them had any idea that what they were doing was unethical. Yet, this type of situation is extremely common at universities today. Even though doctoral degree holders in cybersecurity are not common, almost every university has some type of an offering with the word "cybersecurity" in the offering! Some are even spelling it as two words. Sometimes, a university will list the word with both spellings on their websites and marketing materials! These programs are not necessarily led by cybersecurity degree holders. Many program chairs do not even have doctoral or comparable terminal degrees. The entire goal is revenue - not education!

Between 2013 and 2016 I had turned down the opportunity to teach at UMUC several times due to ethical concerns. When I finally joined in 2016, it was because I had been given the assurance that I would be empowered to implement ethical practices within my program and that the focus would be education and not money! I knew if we focused on the quality of education, actual learning and success of students, and the reputation of the program, money would automatically flow in - and it did at an unprecedented pace during my tenure there.

9.5 CAREFULLY CHOOSE ETHICAL COMPANIES

If a company or its officers are not ethically aligned with our values we may become guilty by association. Within such companies we may be required to perform or overlook unethical and even illegal activities; our personal brands could always be in serious peril. We must always be willing to disassociate ourselves from organizations and people if our values and personal brands are becoming compromised.

Unethical companies will often require unethical and sometimes illegal contractual restrictions on our ability to earn a living; they may try to take away rights to our intellectual property, or even prevent us from working for multiple employers at the same time. No organization should be allowed to have control over all hours of our day if they are only paying us for eight! People with strong personal brands will have a stronger negotiating position in such situations.

In general, we should seek competent legal counsel to make sure contracts are ethical and legal. Contracts must be bilateral and not unilateral! Sometimes an organization will require such contracts after hiring, knowing full well that the employee is in a weaker position after joining - specially if they have resigned from another position. Once I faced such a situation two weeks after starting work at an organization.

The university wanted me to adapt my Master's and Doctoral programs according to their requirements for accreditation. After I had already adapted my Master's program and was about to start the adaptation of the Doctoral program, the university lawyer sent me a whole bunch of legal documents to sign. These documents would essentially hand over ownership rights of my intellectual property to them forever. I would not be able to implement these programs at any other university.

They also insisted on a non-compete agreement, which would prevent me from working for any other university for eighteen months if I left or was terminated for any reason. They also wanted me to sign a document, which would give them the unilateral right to terminate me for any reason or no reason at all! We negotiated for two weeks. However, nothing was negotiable.

I suggested that I give them perpetual rights to use my adaptations. I explained it is like an architect or builder adapting a house design based on a client's needs. The architect or builder remains free to use the same house design and adapt it for another client. In addition, I could never agree to give up my rights to earn a living for any length of time unless they had a provision to compensate me for that length of time.

The organization was adamant about every term in these additional contract documents! In general, hiring organizations have far more power over the relationship after we are hired. This power is frequently abused. The only way to neutralize or successfully defend against this power is to rely on the power of our personal brand, and our financial and emotional independence.

In this case, this organization may have done the same thing successfully with multiple other employees. However, many employees do not bring in substantial amounts of intellectual property. Perhaps they thought I would cave and sign everything since I had already started the job and the position and role came with a lot of prestige and authority.

I was also having a lot of fun and had already recruited students and had even started to market the university during my speaking events. My name, brand, and role were being co-opted to their benefit already. The power situation was clearly in their favor from their point of view.

However, I was turned off by the unethical nature of the documents, the timing, and their refusal to be bilateral about the terms. So, after two weeks of failed negotiations, I resigned.

Since I was about to build groundbreaking programs that would bring in a minimum of $156 million annually, I saw the power situation a little differently. I could not see them implementing the programs without my services. The entire scenario was a warning sign for other crazy things that might happen in the future. The danger to me would be even greater once I adapt the doctoral program and get all the programs running. The university could also terminate me anytime they felt like it. Someone else could take credit for all my work! We should not be supporting such unilateral and unethical arrangements - specially when we are the value producers!

During the entire time, I felt that the executives and the lawyer for the university were being dishonest. This was a serious red flag for me and a warning sign for more of the same. Everyone should be careful about these signs while evaluating job opportunities. They probably did not view it in this manner and insisted they were simply protecting their investment and they were already paying for my services. They viewed my adaptation as a "Work for Hire" - not understanding that the ideas, courses, and the program designs were never theirs to begin with. I was adapting my design for their use.

They should have shown me all required employment documents before I joined, not produce new contracts two weeks after joining! We must always be ready to walk away from these types of hostage nego-tiations. I was able to walk away cleanly because I had maintained my independent health insurance and had not signed up for company spon-sored health insurance. Health insurance is often used by companies to maintain an even higher level of power advantage. Once we can neutral-ize these power advantages, we increase our power.

9.6 AVOID PEOPLE WITH INCONGRUENT PERSONAL BRAND

Just like associating with unethical companies can endanger our per-sonal brands, affiliating with unethical people can do the same damage; guilt by association is real. We should also worry about ethical concerns with journalists and media interviews. I always insist on being able to see the final draft or at least the exact quotes that will be used. Misquotes and out of context attributions can be damaging and it is extremely hard to undo the damage. In addition, I want my name to be displayed accu-rately.

While media exposure is important, we must always remember that they need us more than we need them. So, if media people are unwilling to assure they will quote us accurately or truthfully, we can always turn down the opportunity. This is also why the best interview is usually a written interview. Recorded interviews are also okay. However, we must be incredibly careful of what we say. Anything can be manipulated.

Negative people can also damage or confuse our belief in ourselves. While constructive criticism should always be welcomed, we have nothing to gain from purely personal negative attacks; engaging with these people is unhealthy and will cause bad chemical reactions in our bodies and brains. Negativity is like a cancer; we should never let it spread.

Negative people will always want us to get drawn into their games. They will want to co-opt us into playing their game. However, it is always better to be playing our own game instead of falling into the trap of playing someone else's game. Negative mud-slinging will often make the public think both sides have serious flaws.

This is an area where the laws against lying really need to be strengthened. The fact that lying to the FBI is illegal in the USA but lying to the public or to the press is legal is simply amazing! Until this deficiency is fixed, navigating through this morass will remain challenging for anyone trying to preserve their personal brand value.

The following is a summary of the key points of this section.

LEVERAGING AND PROTECTING PERSONAL BRAND

Compelling Resume and Public Profiles
Negotiate Compensation
Stay In Your Lane
Be Careful of What You Endorse
Carefully Choose Ethical Companies
Avoid People With Incongruent Personal Brand

Leveraging and Protecting Personal Brand

CHAPTER 10

Publishing

Publishing is a key source of power. Publishing is prestigious. It imparts credibility and higher impact to our work, adds significant value to our personal brand, and provides a powerful way to distribute our work globally. Our work can also be added to library collections, cited by others, and used in teaching and learning. Easy cost effective access to publishing is critical for expressing our inner greatness. This chapter is an expanded version of a chapter in my earlier book Cybersecurity Leadership.

10.1 PROBLEMS WITH TRADITIONAL PUBLISHING

The traditional world of publishing has long been controlled by powerful companies with high costs, lofty barriers to access, inaccessible and high priced literary agents as gatekeepers, restrictions on distribution, back room deals and restrictive contracts between publishers and bookstores that deny access to independent publishers, rigid one-sided publishing contracts, and lengthy delays in getting critical information, knowledge, and our message out to a broad global audience.

In this world, except for famous and established authors who have some leverage, the remaining authors control little while publishers control everything. In the academic community, the sad result has been an excessive cost of textbooks. Captive students are forced to buy even black and white paperback books that cost nearly $200! Even though ebook production and distribution costs are far lower, ebook prices are close to paperback prices. Even if someone buys a paperback, there is no provision for a free ebook to carry around on a smartphone or tablet.

Royalties for authors tend to be negligible. Copyright is typically owned by the publishers and authors lose control of their own work. Edit cycles are dependent on the discretion of the publishers and not the desires of the author. Thus, the content can be outdated and stay out-dated for long periods of time.

In the academic world, the situation is even more severe. Authors are required to publish in peer reviewed journals to be considered for tenure. Thus, a cottage industry of journals has sprouted in every dis-cipline. Almost none of them pay the authors anything. They do not pay the peer reviewers either. The author's work is handed over to the publisher for their exclusive distribution and sale. Readers must pay the publisher to read the material and even electronic copies are priced at ex-orbitant prices.

I experienced the problems firsthand when an editor affiliated with a traditional publishing company asked me to contribute an article to a textbook. After I spent two weeks writing and rewriting the article to the editor's requirements, my article was approved. I then received a contract offer, which gave the publisher full ownership of all intellectual property rights permanently -- for the princely sum of $100.

The proposed contract also stipulated that I would be liable for breaches as well as "alleged breaches," and my work could be published without attribution to me. When I asked for a fair and balanced con-tract, the editor offered a take-it-or-leave-it option.

When I wanted to publish my doctoral dissertation to make it avail-able at a reasonable cost to anyone in the world, I found that all tra-ditional routes were skewed toward publishers. Most did not offer any royalty payment. Some sites mentioned royalty payments, but amounts were not clearly identified. Nowhere did I see any information about publishing timelines or how much control I would have.

PROBLEMS WITH PUBLISHING TODAY

Publishers in Control
High Prices for Consumers
Formidable Gatekeepers to Prevent Authors from Publishing
Distributors/Stores Controlled by Publishers
Royalties Skewed in Favor of Publishers
Authors Lose Control of Own Work
Authors Expected to do Substantial Marketing
Slow Edit Cycles
Peer Review Journals Expect Work for Free
Yet Work is Locked Away Behind Expensive Pay Walls
Content Stuck in Bygone Era

Problems with Publishing Today

Once I understood the problems related to traditional publishing, I researched the world of independent publishing and was amazed.

10.2 INDEPENDENT PUBLISHING

Independent publishing allows anyone to publish their work without the use of a traditional publisher. While terms such as "vanity publishing" and "self-publishing" are used to denigrate independent publishing, the benefits of independent publishing are dramatically skewed in favor of the author. I published my doctoral dissertation in 2013 in the form of a paperback and an ebook and the experience was empowering and liberating. In 2014, I published two more books in paperback and ebook formats. Then in 2015, I published an audiobook independently. In 2021, I embarked into the world of hardcover publishing in the hopes that libraries and traditional physical bookstores will carry my books.

10.2.1 Benefits of Independent Publishing

Independent publishing allows authors to retain full control over all aspects of the publishing process. I could prepare the manuscript myself or contract with someone to do it. I could edit the manuscript myself or I could hire people to do it.

I could control the schedule, time to market, pricing, global or regional distribution. I was able to give away free ebooks, enter contests, host events, sell signed copies, and even do my own book tours physically or online. I could even price the books differently in different parts of the world. The best part: I could retain a high proportion of the royalties while maintaining a low price of the book for the reader. Lower prices usually mean more sales!

I also found that I could produce ebooks with active hyperlinks to citations or additional rich content such as videos. The ebook versions of this book and my previously published Cybersecurity Leadership contain many hyperlinks and provide the readers with a rich multimedia experience, which modern readers are likely to expect. Such ebooks give readers a much richer learning experience.

In addition, even though I published the paperback version of the book in black and white format to keep costs down, the ebook could still be in full color. However, traditional publishers are still stuck in the old world and far removed from this innovation. Therefore, they are failing to give their readers better value and experiences by not publishing modern books.

Even their prices of ebooks are so far out of line that they end up selling far fewer books! Their primary methods of maintaining market share has been to maintain lots of gatekeepers and contractual agreements with bookstores to keep out independently published authors. Initially, when Amazon used to have a service called Matchbook, I even made the ebook version of my books free once someone purchased the paperback version; traditional publishers do not do this. Hence, our continuous innovation is likely to continue reducing sales for traditional publishers. Furthermore, their role as gatekeepers is becoming dramatically diminished!

Independently published books are continuously increasing their market share. Bookstores are realizing they are losing market share to online storefronts and adapting. At the same time, instead of being squeezed out, high quality independently published books are increasingly outranking traditionally published books; they are unlikely to disappear anytime soon. With the advent of high quality independently published audiobooks, the competition has become even more fierce.

Over time, traditional publishers have also resorted to cost cutting measures, which have reduced quality. It is quite common now for traditionally published books to have glaring typos and grammatical errors. Even the traditional marketing support for authors has declined significantly. Therefore, traditionally published authors must do a lot of marketing on their own. Otherwise, their books will languish with sluggish sales. Since 2013, I have helped many authors become independent publishers - many had already tried the traditional route and found that they made little or no money and their rights to their own books had been severely curtailed. They could not even produce audio versions of their books unless their publisher agreed and took the initiative!

Look Inside and Audible Sample Options

Amazon's Look Inside book preview option allows buyers to easily figure out the quality of an author's writing. Regardless of the version of the book someone is interest in buying, for books with Audible audiobook versions, there is also an Audible Sample option. This is powerful in leveling the playing field for everyone. Independently published books in newer fields such as cybersecurity have done rather well compared to traditionally published books. At the same time, traditional publishers have responded to pricing and time to market pressures by reducing staff, cutting costs and services, and reducing quality control steps; some have even sought bankruptcy protections to realign their businesses to survive.

Consequently, when typos and errors are discovered, these errors are not usually corrected in a timely manner due to lengthy production cycles. Independent publishers can usually correct errors within a matter of 24 to 48 hours - something I have consistently done for all my books!

If they wish to produce an audio version of their book, they can easily do it themselves or collaborate with an independent audiobook narrator and producer.

Many authors have also suffered drastic consequences and uncertainty when their traditional publishers or agents suddenly went out of business. Some found out too late that their traditional "publisher" was in fact a self-publishing vanity press that charged them a lot of money for producing printed books with severe limitations for producing ebooks, audiobooks, or globally distributing these books! Yet, their rights had been curtailed! Given the powerful technology available today, every prospective author should carefully research independent publishing and marketing options before making a final decision.

 INDEPENDENT PUBLISHING BENEFITS

Authors in Control
Lower Prices for Consumers
No Gatekeepers to Prevent Authors from Publishing
Distribution Mostly Controlled by Authors
Royalties Skewed in Favor of Authors
Authors Retain Control of Own Work
Faster to Market
Fast Edit Cycles
Authors Can Support Open Educational Resources Trend
Content Can Be Rich with Hyperlinks and Media

Independent Publishing Benefits

10.2.2 Publishing eBooks and Print Books

Independent publishing through Amazon's **www.kdp.com** or Ingram's **www.ingramspark.com** are simple and cost effective options for publishing ebooks, paperbacks, and hardbacks while retaining the highest level of control over your work and royalties. Barnes and Nobles also has an independent publishing platform. Ingram can distribute ebooks, paperbacks, and hardbacks through Amazon as well as many other global distributors and sellers. Hardbacks are preferred by libraries and some bookstores and the cost of producing full color hardbacks are now comparable to the cost of producing similar paperbacks.

Both platforms allow Print on Demand options with global distribution. Thus initial setup costs are low; until someone orders a print book, the book is not printed. To maintain a high degree of independence and to avoid vendor lock, authors should clearly define their goals and maintain independent nonexclusive relationships with multiple publishing platforms to meet their goals. The processes are reasonably transparent, and the author knows exactly how the royalty payments will work.

I tried and opted out of the exclusive Kindle Unlimited arrangement because the subscription model and royalty algorithm are skewed heavily towards Amazon and even if thousands of pages of a book are read, authors make pennies, which are not even equivalent to a single sale. However, staying in the arrangement for one cycle can provide some marketing opportunities as this feature allows authors to give away free copies of their ebooks. This can help to obtain reviews and initial reactions.

Except for Amazon's Kindle Unlimited, royalty payments are typically skewed in favor of authors. Authors can choose sales prices and these can be changed at any time. Content can also be changed anytime. Authors can design covers using templates on the platform or upload their own design.

When authors are ready to publish their print books, they can obtain free ISBN numbers from the independent publishing platform of their choice and can have both black and white and color versions of their books at different prices. eBooks on KDP do not require ISBN numbers. Even if you publish ebooks and paperbacks through Amazon, you can publish hardbacks through IngramSpark. The hardback requires a different ISBN anyway, and you can use a free one from IngramSpark. The only drawback of using a free ISBN is that the same ISBN cannot be used to publish through other platforms. Thus, authors should explore if buying their own ISBN makes sense for their independent publishing goals. You can also obtain a free US Library of Congress Control

Number (LCCN) at https://locexternal.servicenowservices.com/auth before you publish your book. You will need an ISBN number in order to apply for an LCCN. Response is usually received in a couple of days.

Both KDP and IngramSpark provide a wide range of tools to simplify the publishing process. IngramSpark even has an HTML editing option for authors with some expertise in HTML. Both platforms have cover creators with plenty of templates, which can be customized to create professional quality covers. For KDP, an application called Kindle Create or a Word template can be downloaded for either Windows or Mac computers to transform any book manuscript into a professional looking book.

Once transformed, you can make further edits before submitting for publication. While creating the book and the cover, use public domain images or images that you created or have purchased rights for. You can change the size and location of images, include image captions and credits, and have text wrapped around the image to give your book a highly professional look. Save your work frequently on IngramSpark as the platform crashed unexpectedly several times while producing hard cover books and I lost unsaved work.

Regardless of platform, always maintain a separate control copy outside of the platform. IngramSpark will strip a lot of formatting as well as Table of Contents. In addition, I could not find an easy way to do Level 3 or higher level headings. However, as you reformat, you will be able to see PDF proofs for chapters, book parts, and the complete book long before you approve it for publication.

Authors using traditional publication methods often spend months or years trying to get their books perfect because changes and editing are hard after initial publication. Independent publishing allows you to change the content any time you want. The new content is available to new purchasers usually within forty eight hours of the update. eBook purchasers can even download updated versions. These updates can be made based on initial performance and reviews of the book.

I had to do major revisions twice within a span of eighteen months for one of my books, in order to improve its quality and relevance. No book is ever perfect when initially published. In the new world of independent publishing, getting the book out sooner is advisable. Initial reader reaction can be vitally important for an author to assess what changes will be required. This is similar to the agile method of software development.

Independent publishing platforms allow authors to track sales in near real time. You can track where in the world the book has sold. You can buy author copies at the cost of production. This will allow you to have your own book signing events, independent book sales, and your own sales and promotion channels. You can gift books, host contests and giveaways and various promotional events. You can sell signed paperback copies from your own website or sales portal. You can even lend your ebook to others.

10.2.3 Publishing Audiobooks

Once the ebook and print versions of your book are done and you have done all the editing and updating that you are likely to do, you can focus on producing an audiobook. Publishing an audiobook version of your book is a powerful way to expand your market and increase the value of your personal brand. This is specially true if you narrate your own audiobook. Author narrated audiobooks connect an author to their listeners in a powerful way. There are plenty of free tools and technologies that will allow you to produce an audiobook independently.

Audiobook Creation Exchange (https://www.acx.com/) is Amazon's marketplace for independent audiobook authors, narrators, agents, and publishers. Audiobooks published through this marketplace can be sold through Audible, Amazon, and iTunes. This is the platform I used to publish the audio version of my book Cybersecurity Leadership in 2015. The audio version of this book was also published on the ACX platform. Almost all typos and errors are usually caught and corrected during an audiobook narration and production process.

ACX.COM - AUDIOBOOK

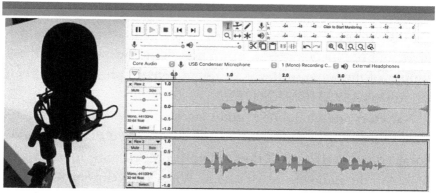

Record, Clean Noise, Edit, Compress, Limit, Normalize, and Amplify to meet ACX Specifications and Upload

Simple Steps for Audiobook Production

I chose to narrate the book myself to maintain authenticity, save costs, and to learn the entire process of producing audiobooks. All requirements are well explained on the site including volume and headroom requirements. The site does not have a cover creation option. Thus, some other image editing tool must be used to produce an exact square cover according to their specifications. If the image is not an exact square, the site will reject it and the process may take a few tries. If your book has disallowed words in its title, you will not be able to use those words on the audiobook cover and will have to substitute spaces or special characters in order to get your audiobook cover approved.

For me, producing the audiobook worked out well because my audiobooks became an inexpensive alternative for people who were unable to attend my university classes. Students also bought the audiobook to review important concepts. The audiobook also helped sell more copies of the ebook and paperback because people wanted to use those as ready references. Audiobooks also increase the accessibility of our work.

Audiobooks have expanded my market dramatically and allowed me to compete at par with traditionally published books. Since many of the traditionally published audiobooks do not have author narration, I actually have a competitive advantage. When a non-subject matter expert narrates a business audiobook, much of the author's intent and passion is lost.

Furthermore, I have been able to offer a separate audiobook narration and production service to support other independent authors. Samples of my audio work can be found here: https://www.acx.com/narrator?p=A29RMCMIQYDYX.

Narrators and audiobook producers need to be extremely careful while auditioning or producing audiobooks on the ACX platform on Royalty Share deals as ACX does not vet people claiming to have rights to publish the audio version of a book. When a Royalty Share deal falls through after all the narration and production work is done, narrators may never get paid for their hard work. I learned this the hard way after producing five audiobooks for scammers. I made no money for several months of work and the audiobooks were pulled from circulation by Audible when they discovered the fraud.

As of right now, they do not require any escrows or good faith money to protect narrators. Every time I contacted them, they asked me to vet Rights Holders myself. Our resources for such vetting are very limited. I did succeed in avoiding a few scams later because the listings and interactions with the purported Rights Holders appeared suspicious and I was able to contact and obtain responses from the real authors. Many authors do not respond even if you contact them through their websites or LinkedIn.

10.2.4 Audio Production and Editing Tools

Even though the thought of producing an audiobook might seem daunting, except for the computer, the process and tools are readily available at low or zero cost. Your goal should be to convert every chapter into an MP3 file. These files can be easily produced using a good quality USB condenser microphone connected to a computer. You will also need pop filters and foam windscreens to reduce unwanted wind noise.

A single chapter does not initially have to be a single MP3 file. Several MP3 files can be combined into a single file during editing. The recordings can have multiple defects, including volume issues, breathing noises, unwanted mispronunciations, sound interruptions and other similar defects. Most of these can be corrected during the audio editing process. Listeners prefer shorter segments and overly large chapters should be broken up into smaller chapters or chapter segments.

For my first audiobook, I used a high quality stereo mixing board, a high quality condenser microphone, and a free open source audio editing software called Audacity (from https://www.audacityteam.org/) to produce the files. However, Audacity also has a recording feature, which can export to an MP3 format. This software has powerful features to clean excessive room noise and other defects that will invariably creep into the recording. Mono sound is preferred in audiobooks. Read and follow the platform's current requirements as well as their helpful guides and videos.

AUDIO EDITING

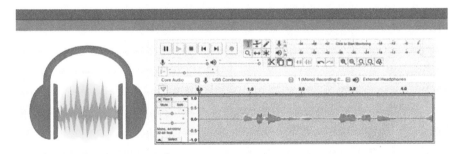

Open source Audacity as a free option

Most computer fans make a lot of noise, which will be picked up by all good microphones. In addition, the sound hardware and drivers of your computer will have a dramatic impact on the quality of your audio recording. Unless they are identical computers, do not ever record different parts of a book on two different computers. I had to redo half of a book because the difference in sound quality was painfully obvious. On one computer most of the bass from my voice had been dropped. After trying multiple computers and laptops, I found Apple's iMac platform with the new M1 chip to produce the best quality sound.

I used YouTube training videos to perform Noise Reduction and sound editing. I corrected recording errors by either rerecording or copying and pasting from a different location. I was also able to rectify volume fluctuations between multiple recording sessions.

The software is amazingly easy to use and I could work on exceptionally fine details by magnifying each section as I worked on them. Editing is a time consuming process. However, the power of having everything within my own control made it well worth it. Loud hissing noises, refrigerator and air conditioner noises will all have to be avoided or cleaned. Too much cleaning will make the voice sound weird. So you must find the right balance. A single 8-hour audiobook can easily take a month to produce due to the lengthy cleaning and editing processes.

After months of experimentation, I found the following steps to be best for audiobooks recorded in my voice. Compress first using the default settings in Audacity. Run the Limiter with a **Hard Limit** and rest at default settings. Finally, Normalize to -3db. After that, depending on initial recording volume, Amplify as needed until ACX specifications are met. Do not over amplify or under amplify and double check that all files sound consistent. You will need high quality computer speakers with a powered subwoofer in order to listen to your recording properly. Additionally, I used a Behringer studio quality headphone set to test how the recording will sound to a typical listener.

ACX requires between .5 and 1 second of ambient Room Noise at the beginning and 1 to 5 seconds at the end of every sound file. While the ACX Upload Manager will check for and alert you to fix all kinds of audio issues, it will not check for headroom. Make certain that every file has this headroom to avoid delays in getting approval for your audiobook.

As of right now, the following audiobooks I have narrated and produced are available globally through Audible. I have provided the Audible USA link information below. However, listeners can visit their regional Audible site and search using a narrator name.

1. Cybersecurity Leadership - this book is about corporate governance and leadership in the digital era.
https://www.audible.com/pd/Cybersecurity-Leadership-Audiobook/B00TYUG82Q

2. Bring Inner Greatness Out - this book is about career success and personal empowerment in the digital era.
https://www.audible.com/pd/Bring-Inner-Greatness-Out-Audiobook/B08V8J8Q4M

3. Lotus Land written by Bhuban Patra - this book is a fantasy fiction set in ancient India.
https://www.audible.com/pd/Lotus-Land-Audiobook/B091517FJQ

4. Neelkanth written by Satyam Srivastava and Rajeev Garg - this book is a crime thriller with philosophical undertones set in modern India.
https://www.audible.com/pd/Neelkanth-Truth-Lies-Deceit-Murder-Audiobook/B0988824B6

5. The Chronicles of Spoony: Volumes 1-3 written by Jim Larsen - this is a PG-13 humorous book that teenagers and adults alike will enjoy.
https://www.audible.com/pd/The-Chronicles-of-Spoony-Vols-1-3-Audiobook/B08W17KTZ7

6. Family Secrets written by Ellie Jay - this is a crime thriller with a sprinkle of sarcasm that teenagers and adults alike will enjoy.
https://www.audible.com/pd/Family-Secrets-Audiobook/B09D5FQ7L5

CHAPTER 11

Book Marketing and Brand Promotion

Once the hard work of producing the books is done, the fun of marketing and accompanying brand promotion can accelerate dramatically. Book promotion and brand promotion are symbiotic activities. Doing one automatically has a positive impact on the other. Some marketing must begin well before the books are published in any format. The following is an example.

LinkedIn Post Prior to Book Publication

For any posts in social media, carefully choose hashtags that will make the post easy to find. Such posts can also be used to engage your community of followers. For example, you can produce different versions of the cover and get feedback from your LinkedIn or other community by allowing them to vote on the cover.

You can also do the same for the title of the book. This engagement will make others invested in your work and success. Similarly, you must also engage in their posts by Liking, Sharing, and Commenting. Social media relationships must be nurtured so that you can derive the full benefit of having a community of followers.

It is better to spend fifteen to thirty minutes each day posting and engaging with your social media network instead of engaging for several hours once a month. Just like any human relationship, frequency of contact will foster a deeper relationship between you and your network.

Relationships are a two way street. As you celebrate the successes of the people in your network, they will celebrate and enhance your success. Over time, you will get to know the people in your network, and you will establish deep relationships with people all over the world. Every relationship will be critical for your brand development and over-all success.

11.1 DISTRIBUTION

The book setup process in Kindle Direct Publishing and In-gramSpark provides easy to use options for free global distribution of your books. I enabled distribution to all Amazon sites globally as I could not think of any reason why I would want to restrict the market. Ama-zon has multiple regional sites, and your book can be priced differently on each site. IngramSpark has similar options and exploring both op-tions is a good idea to avoid vendor lock.

Even though it is simple to peg the price to the US dollar equivalent, in some parts of the world, this price may be too high. For example, an ebook price of $9.99 is considered inexpensive in the USA. However, the equivalent in Indian Rupees, might seem expensive to many people in India. So, I used my knowledge of local economic realities, as much as possible, to price my books globally.

11.2 PROMOTING YOUR BOOKS

Book promotion is another subtle art form. If you are pushy about promoting your book, you will turn off people. Think of your own re-actions when you hear someone promoting a book too obviously. How did you feel? How do you feel about ads? The trick is to share a snip-pet or glimpse of an important message or content that people will learn from the book. It can even be a review of the book. Most of the ideas have already been covered in great detail in the earlier sections of this book. The following summary is particularly relevant to authors.

BOOK PROMOTION

**Speaking at Conferences
Podcasts, Webinars, Interviews
Videos, Websites, Blogs, Merchandise
Book Signing Events
Book Reviews
Entering and Winning Contests
Cross Brand Promotion
Engagement with Supporters**

Book Promotion

This model of promotion is content marketing. As I discussed earlier, it is getting harder and harder for pure ads to generate sales. Such ads may create brand recognition. However, actual sales occur through connection and value creation. That is the modern method of content marketing. I do not recommend buying ads or paid reviews.

Content marketing has also been called the freemium model of sales, whereby a small scale version of a product or a part of it is given away for free to a customer to create affinity for the product. Once customers benefit from the scaled down version of the product, they can generate sales in two important ways: 1) they tell their friends and network about it and provide free brand awareness, and 2) they themselves buy the premium version of the product.

I created videos with slides for the first two chapters of my book Cybersecurity Leadership and uploaded them on YouTube. These videos are used in many schools, colleges, and universities. Therefore, they create awareness and promote the book at no cost to me. Since traditional publishers almost never do this, they are at a serious disadvantage in the modern marketplace and the traditional form of publishing is continuing a steady decline.

Open Educational Resources, Creative Commons materials, and disaggregated digital materials are also replacing textbooks at a rapid pace. In the graduate program I implemented using open resources, each student used to save an average of $400 per term. Furthermore, they received current learning materials for their learning topics in every course under my jurisdiction. Additionally, each topic was covered at the right level for the problem the student had to solve. Thus, students were not overwhelmed with unnecessary reading or extraneous materials. Typical textbooks can never do justice to the learning needs of all classes at thousands of learning institutions globally. As more universities adopt properly curated and custom written materials for their academic programs, it becomes a competitive advantage for the university's program. This was certainly true for my program and I touted this distinction during my marketing efforts to recruit students.

11.2.1 Conferences

Speaking at conferences is one of the best ways to promote books as well as personal brands. The presentation can be about any topic - ideally unrelated to the book. However, the bio, the cover slide, and the last slide are usually great places for subtle promotion of books. Direct and obvious book or other product sales from the lectern or the presentation stage can be a turn off for the audience and deadly for the presenter.

Example of Promo for Cybersecurity Marketing Conference 2021
Cybersecurity Marketing Society

Conferences will promote speakers and create marketing materials for speakers to use and these materials will not only promote the event, but also the speaker and their books and services for a long time before and after the event. These are powerful!

Speaking at too many events can dilute someone's personal brand specially if the topic of discussion is the same. While some free speaking engagements may be required to gain initial name recognition, high quality speakers rarely speak for free. Every speaker should view public speaking as work and should expect to get paid for the work.

Speakers are the main reason anyone attends a conference. They expect to learn and gain value from the event, specially if they are paying to attend. Therefore, at the very least conferences should waive registration fees and cover expenses for speakers with strong personal brand value as these speakers will sell tickets.

Why would you sell tickets for a conference organizer without any compensation? Most conference organizers are for profit organizations. Many are highly compensated by vendors who will be attempting to sell to the attendees. Therefore, vendors or organizers should be sponsoring your work as a speaker; there must be some tangible benefit to you as a speaker. Even a display table for your books or a book signing event, can be a tangible benefit.

Therefore, it is important to figure out how many tickets you are likely to sell for the organizers. A good starting point of negotiations for high quality speakers is roughly five times the value of a ticket. You can also set a price for for-profit organizations and a different price for non-profit organizations. Even government organizations have a budget for speakers.

Keynote speakers are almost always paid well as they may be the main attraction for an event and likely to generate hundreds of ticket sales. Since my speaking engagement always includes a high level of promotion for the event where I am speaking, the conference invariably sells many extra tickets.

Speakers being paid to speak must be specially careful not to promote their own books during the presentation. Book covers on the cover slide and the last slide are okay but promotion of the book during the presentation is almost never okay unless the presentation is about the book itself.

Every speaker needs to realize that once they appear credible and value laden during a presentation or speaking engagement, audience members will invariably want to know more about the speaker's work.

Every speaking event will result in additional opportunities. However, if you continue to give away your work for free, it may become difficult to get paid speaking opportunities later.

11.2.2 Table Displays and Book Signing Events

Book signing events, table displays for books, and general networking with the conference attendees can generate significant amounts of sales and additional connection with the audience members. Sometimes, if the organizers of a conference are paying a reduced speaking fee or cannot afford to pay a speaking fee, a speaker should negotiate a free display table for book and merchandise sales.

If the display table is in conjunction with a keynote speaking opportunity, then the display table can be an excellent sales and networking opportunity. Published authors should welcome the opportunity to do book signings. I personalize books with a message and then sign them. This creates another personal connection. Once I even saw a social media post by someone celebrating the 5th anniversary of meeting me and getting the signed book! The power of a genuine human connection is incredible.

Display tables are fabulous opportunities to build connections with our audience members. Many will have follow-up questions. Some will want to buy a signed book as a memento of the event or the meeting. These table displays must be carefully thought out. Simply displaying books is one option. However, when we take the time to decorate and trick out the display using imagination and innovation, our efforts will be dramatically rewarded. Whenever I took some awards and placed them on the display tables, they invariably generated interest and questions. The resulting conversations created opportunities for relationships. The awards also imparted a high level of credibility and generated more student leads and book sales.

Baltimore Book Festival, 2019

The conversations turned more interesting because none of the competitor table displays had comparable props. Therefore, we had more foot traffic and the differences in quality and perceived value were rather starkly apparent! If one university display table is full of awards, while another has nothing - not even a credible faculty member, which university would you pick? If you are able to talk with a credible faculty member who answered your academic questions and offered to become your mentor in the discipline of your interest at one table, but could only talk to a marketing assistant with brochures at another, which university would you pick? I remember many times, the marketing person had to call me back to the display table to talk with a prospective student who eventually joined the program.

Recruiting students, particularly at the graduate level, is an extremely high touch activity! Too many students aren't even in the market until they meet someone who inspires them and points out the possibilities in their lives! Students will pick a university where they know that the academic program leaders will be engaged in their success.

If the person they meet has a strong personal brand and has authored books in the field, the program appears even more credible. A typical marketing person can never do this.

Poorly run online academic programs have developed such a bad reputation that most working professionals would not even consider them until they see that such programs can win awards against traditional programs and can be better in quality. For every award I won, I had to compete against all types of universities and contestants to win!

Since I was promoting the academic program I was personally running, I could look people in the eye and boldly tell them, "You will be joining the highest quality program in the world and I will personally take care of you. If you do the work, you will succeed." Such a statement coming from the Chair of a program with personal accomplishments and student testimonials to back them up is powerful! I usually took 15 minutes to evaluate someone's academic background and career goals and recommend a credible path for success. No marketing person or ad can ever do this!

Author's Corner Table at CISSE 2018

Keynote Speaker Display Table at ARMA Infocon 2019, Nashville, TN

I always take lots of photos at every event. These photos depict stories, and these stories are priceless personal brand promotion opportunities! More pictures and stories mean more book and brand promotion; and these promotional artifacts have an exceptionally long shelf life! They are far better than any chintzy TV ad - which wastes money and diminishes a university's academic credibility.

Selling university programs is simply not the same as selling a tube of toothpaste! Students join academic programs because of the credible faculty they will learn from! People affiliate with people - not organizations. Faculty with strong personal brands must recognize their own product value and ensure that they get a fair share of the money they bring in. Once everyone can build strong personal brands, the days of exploited faculty - specially the most dramatically exploited adjunct faculty - will be over! People need to claim back their power!

11.2.3 Book Giveaways and Contests

Conferences are also great opportunities for book giveaways. Such book giveaways and signings can be sponsored by organizers, exhibiting vendors, or your own sponsor. Sponsors can place stickers inside a book stating Compliments of XYZ. Their small investment in your book suddenly gives them lasting marketing value with a long shelf life. People throw away marketing materials they pick up at conferences, but they will not throw away a book and will refer to it from time to time.

Contests are another fun and powerful way to promote personal brands as well as generate book sales. These contests can be for anything that you are qualified to win. Even if you never win, the contest gives you the opportunity to let your network know you are a contender. The entire period of the contest can be used effectively as a content marketing tool.

You can also host book giveaways or enter the book into contests. You can create short one to two minute videos seeking votes and create even more buzz around your personal brand and books. A single book giveaway contest can result in several hundred entries - many of whom will end up buying the book once the contest is over.

(ISC)2 Congress Florida Bookstore - 2016

11.2.4 Book Festivals

Book festivals are particularly important for independent authors. At such events, promotion of the book and author is more important than sales. Participation alone creates a higher level of credibility for the author and the book. During book festivals, we must interact with all the visitors and build relationships. Networking with other independent authors is also critical as all independent authors can amplify each other's voices during social media promotions. In addition, cross following and helping everyone gain more connections and followers will multiply the impact even further!

I participated in the Baltimore Book Festival for several years and the exposure was excellent. To reduce costs, multiple authors can team up to rent a single tent or display table. This also increases the likelihood of more traffic to the stall. I partnered with other authors for a couple of years and it was always helpful to have company and various personalities to interact with the public.

Baltimore Book Festival 2019

While most book festivals charge a fee for a display table, there are an incredible number of free or low cost opportunities for similar displays. Sometimes, a homeowners association or an organization such as Rotary International or MENSA will allow free participation with a table display or even a speaking opportunity. During participation, you need to use creative marketing ideas to generate interest and drive traffic to your booth. At the 2019 Baltimore Book Festival, I placed my banner with my picture holding the $(ISC)^2$ ISLA award guitar in front of the Baltimore Harbor. This picture has always generated interest and questions.

Most people would never have thought to take a picture with this guitar or to make a banner featuring this picture. However, this level of creativity and risk taking is precisely what makes anyone stand out! As one of my friends once told me, "While others are simply going fishing, you are out to reel in marlins!" While I never thought of it that way until my friend mentioned it, that's how we need to think. Once we achieve something, we need to think of the next level of greatness.

We need to think like no one else will. This process is also my style of changing the game regularly. The goal should always be to be the sole player in a game - victory is always assured when no one else can play the game we just created. In most cases, playing someone else's game that is already rigged against us makes no sense! While there are risks associated with this approach, the rewards are proportionately just as great!

My creative thinking after arriving at the festival and figuring out how to best use the marketing and brand promotion opportunity were critical in making the event more successful. The banner created a huge amount of interest as people examined and read the banner, turned and then jumped in surprise when they saw me in the booth opposite! We made the experience memorable for them! They may even talk about it with others. That is the idea!

Pre and post marketing pictures of the event are huge opportunities for brand promotion. I usually take pictures with all friends who come to the event, share it with them and use them strategically to tell stories about the event. Stories of an event can live long after the event is over. If a friend shares a picture or story about the event, even better!

Sometimes we can get a speaking slot at a book festival. Members of the media might visit or take pictures for additional earned media marketing. At times, random visitors will be so intrigued that they will want to take a picture with the author. These are priceless and we should embrace every one of these opportunities! Every time people share pictures, we get free advertising and the possibility of book sales.

11.2.5 Sponsorships

Sponsors can support a speaker's presentation or webinar to collect leads and be acknowledged in the slides, conference agenda, and website. Once again, this form of subtle promotion without turning off anyone is highly effective. Sponsoring a competent professional speaker and educator to provide a value packed presentation is far better than a vendor executive paying tens of thousands of dollars to make an infomercial from the speaker stage.

Vendor related speakers talking mostly about their products, invariably turn people off as the attendees may have paid significant money to register for the event and came to learn; they are not interested in listening to infomercials. Sometimes they need continuing education credits and may sit through the presentations but will be inattentive and scrolling through their smartphones.

Instead, the value from a sponsor logo in the slides of an educational presentation by a professional speaker and thought leader with a credible personal brand, can last for years and be shared around by lots of people all over the world. Even sponsored webinars and online events can have a dramatic level of lasting marketing value compared to a conference booth.

11.2.6 Book Reviews

Book reviews are critical. Books that have more than a hundred reviews tend to be promoted by Amazon and Audible - specially if the average review is higher than four. To achieve this, I had to give away several hundred ebooks and audiobooks for free.

I did not have to spend any money to do this. Audible helped me by giving me a hundred free audiobooks to give away in the US market and another hundred to give away in the UK market. My global network helped me give away all these free books to people in their networks and then helped me gain more than a hundred reviews on both Amazon and Audible.

Positive reviews can be used for additional marketing purposes. Such reviews can help an author point to someone else's experience with the book without expressly suggesting a purchase. This is a little more subtle. Similarly, news pieces about the book or the author can be powerful too.

Library   Wish List   Plans & Pricing   Browse ∨

Business & Careers > Workplace & Organizational Behavior

Cybersecurity Leadership
Powering the Modern Organization

By: Mansur Hasib
Narrated by: Mansur Hasib
Length: 7 hrs and 11 mins
Unabridged Audiobook
Release date: 02-25-15
Language: English
Publisher: Tomorrow's Strategy Today, LLC
☆ ☆ ☆ ☆ ☆ 4.3 (119 ratings)

Cybersecurity Leadership on Audible

All reviews do not have to be positive. Even the best books will never have 100% positive reviews. Therefore, it is particularly important for any author not to engage or comment on any negative review. Such engagement from supporters may be okay but in general an author's engagement in negative reviews does not reflect well on the author.

If the negative review is constructive and points out flaws that are easily fixable, the author should fix those issues. I fixed all the issues I could possibly fix. In some cases, the reader was looking for a technical book even though the description clearly stated that my book was about people and leadership and not about technology.

An early reviewer of the first edition of one of my books wrote a bad review because that edition had too many typos. So, I painstakingly fixed all the typos in the book within six months. Another reviewer wanted an index. So, I added an index. During the marketing and discussion of the first edition of my book Cybersecurity Leadership, I recognized additional chapters that needed to be written. I also recognized several redundant chapters that needed to be consolidated.

Buzz, sentiments, discussions, reviews, and sales are all used by various sites to rank ebooks, print books, and audiobooks. We should also try to get books into libraries by donating copies to them or requesting county or city public libraries to get them. We can track library holdings in Worldcat: https://www.worldcat.org/title/cybersecurity-leadership-powering-the-modern-organization/oclc/881738909

While Goodreads is a reasonable site for reviews, there does not appear to be much vetting on whether the reader actually purchased or read the book. At times an author will get spurious reviews from competing authors with their own books to peddle. In addition, the practice of allowing ratings without a substantive review by most sites has watered down the credibility of reviews. Initially, Amazon used to require some text to go with a rating, but now they have discontinued this, much to the distress of authors. Furthermore, a cottage industry of paid reviewers has cropped up using a variety of schemes to get authors to pay for reviews. Thus, spurious ratings are now fairly common. Text reviews remain useful.

Authors must remember that authentic reviews are not paid for. While it is okay for an author to send a complimentary copy of a book or audiobook in the hopes of getting a review, it cannot be a quid pro quo. Authors need to be vigilant in ensuring their community of actual readers and supporters do post reviews to balance out spurious ratings.

However, any website with a review of our book will be helpful in generating sales and interest in both the author and the books. We should collect all helpful links and provide cross links on our own websites.

11.2.7 Merchandise

Personally branded merchandise such as T-shirts, mugs, and other gifts or mementos as giveaways, raffles, or even purchase can dramatically enhance the credibility and perceived value of our personal brands. These are all part of packaging. Good packaging always enhances the perceived value of any product.

I made #DrCybersecurity T-shirts in both men's and women's sizes and three colors due to popular demand. I made both T-shirts customizable with any of my quotes. I was fascinated to see people wearing these T-shirts with pride at conferences! Sites such as Vistaprint are great places for high quality inexpensive business cards, banners, T-shirts, and other marketing materials that can be shipped directly to a purchaser. I used Namebadge to produce custom name tags with logos and custom lettering at a decent price.

#DrCybersecurity T-Shirt Sample

11.3 RESULTS

While I have shared some results in the earlier sections of this book, let me provide a glimpse into some additional results I experienced. First, a couple of words have become synonymously associated with my name and work. Whenever the words "cybersecurity leader" and "cybersecurity leadership" are searched my work will show up. In addition, if I start to search for "cybersecurity leader" Google's typeahead feature suggests my book on the topic.

Google Search Type Ahead Results Example

If I search for "cybersecurity leadership" my book and profile are highly likely to be displayed on the first page. This is powerful and can be achieved through sheer personal brand strength - at no cost. Companies must pay serious money to get similar results with ads. Yet ads rarely have the same impact as an unpaid search result!

Google Search Results on August 20, 2021 (Excluding Paid Ads)

I learned that personal brand, book quality, promotion by author, authentic reviews, book contests, and promotion by the social network of an author, can dramatically improve book sales. Cybersecurity Leadership was nominated twice for the Cybersecurity Canon - a list of must read cybersecurity books originally established as an initiative by Palo Alto Networks and taken over by Ohio State University in August of 2020: https://icdt.osu.edu/cybercanon

It was first nominated to the Cybersecurity Canon by Dawn-Marie Hutchinson in October 2016

https://blog.paloaltonetworks.com/2016/10/the-cybersecurity-canon-cybersecurity-leadership-powering-the-modern-organization/

Damon Ross nominated the book a second time in November 2016: https://blog.paloaltonetworks.com/2016/11/cybersecurity-canon-cybersecurity-leadership-powering-modern-organization/

In 2017, it contended in a global voting contest and won second place. My book has competed well against all types of published books. It has been sold in every continent all over the world. In 2018, three years after its initial publication, the audio version of Cybersecurity Leadership was rated the best cybersecurity audiobook of all time, beating out all traditionally published audiobooks worldwide!

Number One Ranking by Book Authority During 2018

Since then, Book Authority has consistently ranked all versions of Cybersecurity Leadership among the bestselling and best rated cyber-security books of all time. In addition, it is listed among the best cy-bersecurity books of all time at various other international sites such as https://meetcyber.net/bloghome/library and https://www.cyberse-curity-professionals.com/post/cybersecurity-leadership-powering-the-modern-organisation-a-review. It is also used as required and recommended reading at many colleges and universities worldwide and cited in scholarly publications and blogs.

The book is also listed among the best management and leadership books of all time by Book Authority with plenty of traditionally pub-lished books ranked well below it.

Number 30 Ranking Among Best Management Audiobooks of All Time by Book Authority on August 20, 2021

Cybersecurity Professionals based in the United Kingdom published a comprehensive review on October 28, 2020 and posted it on their website: https://www.cybersecurity-professionals.com/post/cybersecu-rity-leadership-powering-the-modern-organisation-a-review. The re-view states: "...This book contains all you need to know about leadership. Leadership is one of the key skills within cybersecurity. We set culture within organisations, and within our own teams too. This book highlights many of the skills that make strong leadership. It does an excellent job of exploring why some set ups were so successful. A key part of this realisation, is to appreciate that there are multiple dimensions to this leadership and being ethical is one of these. ..."

It was one of the books reviewed and highlighted in Tripwire for World Book Day in April of 2021 by Ambler T. Jackson.

Ambler T. Jackson | @AMBLERJACKSON | (LINKEDIN)

In Cybersecurity Leadership: Powering the Modern Organization, author Mansur Hasib does a great job of providing an academic and historical perspective of cybersecurity, including its evolution and what it is, and what it is not. While maintaining that cybersecurity leadership is a business discipline, and not a technology discipline, the author offers several examples that demonstrate the multi-disciplinary and multi-dimensional approach that is necessary to achieve effective cybersecurity leadership. This is a great book for business executives and individuals seeking the role of Chief Information Officer (CIO), or Chief Information Security Officer (CISO). The book's content provides a practical lens through which leaders should view cybersecurity.

The author weaves in the history of cybersecurity, cybersecurity teaching, training and awareness models, historical references to leadership, including historical figures who were considered ethical leaders, and connects the dots between types of leaders and types of leadership, and the narrower topic of cybersecurity leadership. Throughout the book, you will read very simple and practical definitions of leadership, as well as examples of what constitutes good leadership and bad leadership.

In addition to those who aspire to the role of CIO, the book is a practical resource for individuals who may be responsible for serving in an advisory role to the CIO or who would like to understand how to successfully collaborate with the current CIO within their organization. The book includes high-level information related to developing a cybersecurity program, as well as some very specific recommendations related to education, healthcare, and technology. I like that the author focused on the evolution of the CIO's role from an operational one to a strategic one, and I think those individuals participating in the CIO or CISO hiring process will appreciate the discussion of salary negotiations and reporting structures.

Review of Cybersecurity Leadership by Ambler T. Jackson for World Book Day 2021
Tripwire

These results have been obtained without spending money on ads, reviews, or marketing. I simply followed personal branding and marketing ideas I have shared candidly in this book. Of course, I consistently analyzed results of any effort and recalibrated accordingly. I have also innovated and searched for additional ways to grow my brand and market my books and will do so perpetually.

In January of 2021, I also started offering audiobook narration and production services to other authors primarily to create powerful cross brand promotion partnerships. These collaborations are a win win for everyone; other authors gain sales from my marketing and I gain sales due to their marketing.

CHAPTER 12

Final Thoughts

Although I have shared many ideas, experiments, and experiences for you to consider, your own journey will be unique and different. Prioritize ideas and develop your own plan and schedule for actions.

12.1 STOLE OF GRATITUDE

As you may have noted from the ideas and stories I have shared so far, your journey to greatness will be accelerated by several elements, which may include formal education, certifications, membership in clubs and organizations, books, articles, videos, or lab work. However, one of the most important elements of your journey will be mentors, coaches, and sponsors.

Such helpful people will dramatically accelerate your journey. You will need to look for them and make them integral parts of your journey. These three roles are quite different, and you will need various approaches to find them, explore matches, and establish supporting relationships that work for you and all the helpful people in your life.

12.1.1 Mentor

Mentors are usually more experienced and successful people and may have already established their greatness, expertise, personal brand, and reputation in the field; their field will most likely align with your own goals and they are most likely to be able to provide qualified career advice to you every now and then. Qualified mentors are extremely important because unqualified mentors will hamper your journey. This role should not take much time for the mentor; in most cases this is a voluntary role.

Professors or other members of your clubs or networking groups are great candidates to be your mentor. Since you already have a basis for a relationship, and both of you are likely to know about each other, establishing a mentor mentee relationship is easy. In such cases, the mentor may even have a strong interest in seeing you succeed. Once established, these symbiotic relationships can continue long after the formal organizational relationships are terminated. Most of my mentees are current or former students, and graduates from my academic programs.

As you study and learn, you will be inspired by someone's work and may have some questions or ideas surrounding that person's work. Most scholars and experts in any field will welcome short quick questions about their work - specially if you demonstrate that you have read their work. Conference speakers will almost always welcome questions or comments related to the presentation they made. These discussions could become the genesis of a mentor-mentee relationship.

No one has the time or ability to mentor lots of random people for no compensation. You must research and review the work of a prospective mentor. If your questions are already answered in a scholar's written or video recorded works, your questions will not be well received. If someone has written books and you have not read these, asking them to mentor you for free will appear presumptuous and you may lose that connection forever.

Mentors do not teach. Do not ask a mentor to spend hours teaching you anything. That is not how mentorship works. Do not mistake mentoring with coaching, which involves a deeper commitment and longer hours spent in understanding you, teaching you, or refining your skills at something specific. For a successful mentoring relationship, you must have products and ideas and simple short occasional questions. Mentors can then help you.

12.1.2 Sponsor

A sponsor is a mentor on steroids! Sponsors will champion the work and talents of their mentees; sponsors have deeper insight and understanding of the talents of a mentee and believe in them so much that they are willing to put their own reputation and personal brand on the line to lobby for their mentees. This usually happens when a mentee is consistently taking initiative, delivering, and executing on higher and higher levels of excellence and the mentor can trust that the mentee will be reliable. Mentors will not open doors if mentees do not take the initiative to walk through them!

I was not even aware of this term until Tomiko Evans mentioned a video she had come across where this term was explained. After seeing the video, she exclaimed that even though I started out as her mentor, at some point I became her sponsor as I introduced her around, shared her work with others, opened doors, and even lobbied on her behalf. I watched the video, and we had a great discussion around the concept.

I then examined my relationships with my mentees and realized that when my mentees showed a reliable track record of execution based on my suggestions and had demonstrated initiative, originality, discipline to prepare, and the courage to take risks, I would suggest higher goals, point out opportunities, help them write proposals, and also lobby for them to be given a particular challenge or opportunity. In some cases, I nominated them for awards. This is how I became a sponsor for some of my mentees!

Sponsors are great as references also. Sponsors lend credibility to the mentee's work and people in the sponsor's network are likely to take a chance on the mentee. Sponsors do put their own credibility on the line. So before asking for someone to sponsor you for an opportunity, make sure you really want it and will execute properly if given the opportunity.

Sponsors are not simply nominators. While a nomination is an act of sponsorship, nominators are far less invested in the situation. Sponsors on the other hand, may be involved at a far deeper level; they may lobby for you with the selection committee. They have deeper insights about you and may represent your skills and abilities with others. So, make sure your sponsors have accurate information and not false or inflated information. Misrepresentation can destroy a valuable relationship.

12.1.3 Coach

Coaches help you with specific skills and assignments. For example, if you must develop a humorous speech, a coach may help you prepare for that speech. This can entail a series of meetings, discussions, rehearsals, video recordings, analyses, revisions, and detailed feedback. In other words, coaching is usually very time consuming.

For this type of service, although it will be more efficient, you do not need to have read your coach's previous writings. Since you are paying for most of this work, your coach may be fine billing you for the hours it will take for them to bring you up to speed. To coach you properly, they may need to do research, explore your strengths, weaknesses, and ideas at a deeper level. They may need to maintain notes and documentation related to these coaching sessions.

While many mentors will voluntarily provide coaching services at no cost, be careful about demanding or even expecting such services for free. If you can pay for the coaching, you may find that paying your mentor to coach or tutor you on a particular assignment or project creates a far more ethical and mutually rewarding relationship. If teaching is someone's profession, unless they are already being paid by an organization and you are a student there, would it be ethical for you to ask for free teaching services? The key is to understand that you should never exploit someone's good nature.

Everyone must make a living, and no one can provide all services for free to anyone. Coaching requires keen observation and detailed actionable feedback. Coaches are usually seasoned experts in the field. Sometimes, they are retired from the field or not practicing at the level you are. However, they have the experience and expertise to give you trustworthy advice and help you avoid pitfalls. Most new executives benefit greatly from having a former executive or even a current more experienced executive as a coach.

Having a coach does not mean you are not an expert. Regardless of your level of expertise, a coach can be immensely helpful and far more likely to notice finer details in your execution that you will never pick up on. For example, even star baseball players have coaches. Their coaches will usually know what is normal for their players. They will know how to challenge and upskill someone. They might be able to add a new skill to a player's arsenal.

It is completely possible for a mentor to become a sponsor and provide coaching at no cost at their own discretion. However, you as a mentee need to know the difference and do your part faithfully for the relationship to work in your favor. Be ethical in your requests. Barter services or share and promote the services of your mentor in return.

Just like any normal human being, a mentor will always appreciate non-monetary rewards such as thank you notes, posts, celebratory messages, and pleasant surprises. I had such a surprise during Commencement 2018. I was volunteering at the event and suddenly someone mentioned that a graduating student was looking for me. So, I quickly started to go down the student line-up area to see if I could spot any of my students. Suddenly, I saw Tomiko Evans. She handed me a folded piece of yellow silk cloth.

It was the Stole of Gratitude! As a pioneer graduate of my award winning inaugural graduate program, she had asked the administration to allow me to speak at her commencement for five minutes, but she had been turned down. So, she asked the office what else she could do to express gratitude to someone at the university who had helped her most in her academic journey. They suggested the Stole of Gratitude!

The thoughtfulness behind this gesture was priceless to me. Receiving the Stole of Gratitude from a graduating member of the very first cohort of the new and innovative program I had launched was a huge honor for me! I had been nervous about the program; I often wondered if I had made the program too difficult. To receive the Stole of Gratitude from a graduating student from the inaugural class who had experienced all kinds of problems at launch and throughout her academic journey, since they were the first students in every class, was an amazing honor. It also validated that the program was achieving its goal exceptionally well.

**Receiving the Stole of Gratitude from Master of Science Graduate
Tomiko Evans, May 30, 2018**

To this day, I wear the Stole of Gratitude with pride every time I wear my regalia. Watching Tomiko Evans blossom from a graduate student with promise into a dynamic leader in the field, who believes in herself, has been an awesome journey for me. I still joke with her that students who contact me to complain get to have me as a mentor!

12.2 GET YOUR SHOW ON THE ROAD NOW!

Now that you have gone through this book, it is time for you to take your own show on the road. You should summarize my thoughts and ideas you plan to embrace as bullet points for yourself to use and apply - even if for one week at a time. If you try to assimilate all ideas at once, it may seem overwhelming. However, take one idea at a time and spend one week operationalizing that idea.

The book is already organized so you can do everything systematically. However, develop a plan and self-check the areas you have addressed and incorporated in your action plan and timeline. Prepare a realistic action plan and schedule. You could even create a study group or team up with a buddy, do the work, and constructively critique yourselves. That will make it fun and everyone will progress faster.

Dr. Tami Erickson, a regular attendee of my Conversations With #DrCybersecurity video podcast, summarized the ideas I shared in eighteen episodes into fifteen sticky notes. She then organized them into five clusters and operationalized one idea per week over fifteen weeks. I had a fabulous conversation with Dr. Erickson around her sticky notes!

I am sharing the fifteen topics with you. You could create your own set of sticky notes from this book and organize, prioritize, and apply them in the order that makes sense for your situation. Many of the following ideas will be in your plan.

Cluster One:

- Create Trust
- Build Relationships
- Innovation

Cluster Two:

- The CEO is the Brand
- Knowledge and Members of Your Community Are Your Brand
- You Are as Smart as Your Network
- Cross Brand Promotion

Cluster Three

- Continuous Improvement
- It Won't Be Perfect

Cluster Four:

- Think Differently
- Compete on Value
- Make It Fun!

Cluster Five:

- Quit Talking About Problems; Focus on Solutions
- Be Part of the Solution
- What Are You Trying to Achieve?

A thirty three minute video from a keynote presentation I made to Maryland students and educators about Personal Brand also provides a short summary of many of the principles and techniques shared in this book. Go over these principles multiple times and create affinity groups where you can discuss and practice the principles together. Discussions and group work will accelerate everyone's progress dramatically.

Even though a single bull is powerful, a herd of bulls charging in the same direction in synchrony is deadly. Therefore, as more people embrace and capitalize on their personal brands and refuse to work for unethical compensation levels or under unethical contracts, the power will

242 - DR. MANSUR HASIB

start to shift back to the individuals. However, initially, the people with command over their personal brands will have immense power.

If you decide to create a non-profit or similar organization to make the collective of empowered people more effective, it could become a powerful professional association without the restrictions of a worker's union. If you do not take charge of your destiny, the current situation will perpetuate and progressively become worse. Change is never led by the people who are benefiting from the status quo!

I hope this book has revealed to you that we are collectively responsible for the perpetuation of the unethical compensation structure prevalent today. Everything happened so slowly, so incrementally, and over such a long time that everything seemed normal. We perpetuated it by continuing to accept lower and lower levels of compensation because we felt we had no choice. I was among those as well until I recognized the craziness: people bringing in no money, are making far more money than any of the people bringing in the money. Yet, we are the ones treated as expenses!

You must recognize that while we did not have a choice in the past, technology has changed everything and now we have an unbelievable number of tools and choices to build our personal brands and create multiple sources of income in order to gain more control over our time, money, and destiny. The key is to have a plan and continuously experiment, monitor results, and calibrate until you find your stride and your voice. Your final voice will be your own. You will have used ideas from this book as well as others. You will experiment with your own originality and calibrate the level of vulnerability you can comfortably handle. Confronting the truths of your life will not be easy.

You will need to remember that too much at one burst can be overwhelming for both you and your audience. So, bring it out slowly starting with little drips and then progress to a steady stream. Your own comfort level will grow as you continue to do it. Eventually, you will be so comfortable with your greatness that you will transform to a far better version of you than you ever imagined possible; yet it will feel normal! You will wonder how it happened. It will feel like magic.

It will be like learning to drive a car. Your inner greatness is like a car. It is powerful and has many features. It even has cruise control and autopilot! You will need to learn about all its features and how to work all of them in harmony. If you accelerate to top speed without learning to use all the controls and safety features, and how to navigate all the turns, stop signs, and red lights so you can reach your destination safely, you will face a higher probability of crashing and burning.

Go slow. Accelerate safely. Be a safe defensive driver and follow all the rules and you will reach your destination; you will enjoy the immense rewards of your hard work and achievements. The best part of your life is ahead of you. *You cannot change the past, but you can define your future.* There is no end to your greatness. The journey is the destination. *Do not look for a pot of gold at the end of the rainbow; ride the rainbow forever!*

BRING INNER GREATNESS OUT: PERSONAL BRAND

You Do Not Need to be Perfect;
You Need to Perfect Your Uniqueness.

Do Not Look for a Pot of Gold at the End of the Rainbow;
Ride the Rainbow Forever!

#RideTheRainbow

CPSIA information can be obtained
at www.ICGtesting.com
Printed in the USA
JSHW040803220222
23190JS00001B/8